Golden Years

of

HUDDERSFIELD

TRUE NORTH BOOKS
DEAN CLOUGH
HALIFAX
WEST YORKS
HX3 5AX
TEL. 01422 344344
WWW.NOSTALGIA-BOOKS.CO.UK

First published in Great Britain by:
True North Books, Dean Clough, Halifax HX3 5AX
1998

ISBN 1 900 463 77 6

This book is published in association with:

Armitage & Sons Limited

Golden Years of Huddersfield

Text	*Diane Harpwood*
Text pages design	*Mandy Walker*
Photographs compiled by	*Phil Holland*
Cover design	*Mark Smith*
Business development	*Stuart Glenholmes*

Contents

Acknowledgments

The publishers would like to thank

Morris Bray, Trevor Brennan, Neville Brewis,
Martin Hather, Ray Hoyle, Donald Sykes, Ian Thomas,
Ben Whittaker

A 1953 view over St George's Square with the railway station in the background.

Introduction

Producing another book of nostalgic reflections on the Huddersfield we used to know was a challenge taken up enthusiastically by everyone involved.   Where possible we have tried to concentrate upon a period within the memory of most of our readers; the 1940s, 50s and 60s - decades which saw tremendous changes in the town, and a time when there were changes in the world of work, entertainment, public health and retailing. *Change* takes place constantly in every town and Huddersfield is no exception. As we all get older it is often easier to 'step back' and view events and developments with a clearer sense of perspective. Our aim has been to assist in this respect by presenting a 'catalyst' capable of rekindling memories of days gone by in an entertaining manner. Looking through the pages of this book it may be surprising how much change has taken place, and over such a relatively short period, relative to the long history of the area. Street scenes are not neglected. Photographs of this nature were popular in the last book, and understandably so. The changing face of the town is reflected in the way our roads and shops have developed to meet the changing needs of our lives over the years. These photographs show the shops and motorcars we remember from our early days, along with the fashions which were all the rage when we were younger. All combine to refresh our memories of days gone by, and when that occurs the book will have achieved its aim.

Events & Occasions

Inset: Soot blackened but still elegant, the fine building which is Huddersfield's railway station. No prizes for guessing when this photograph was taken! To gain a true impression of the size and scale of these decorations, it is necessary to stand in front of the station and gaze up at the height of the pillars and the width of the facade. This building was once described as a stately home with trains in it! Sir John Betjeman said it was, 'possibly one of the finest examples of British Railway Architecture outside London.' Locally quarried sandstone from Crosland Moor forms the fabric of the building which was completed in 1850. The construction of the railway station marked the beginning of a new period in the development of the town centre which resulted in the many fine buildings we see today, the Town Hall was built in 1875-76. Cleaning in recent years has restored the station to its original beauty and Huddersfield people can feel justly proud of their major landmark, a building of national importance.

The early 1950s and a wave of optimism swept the country. The war was well behind us, 1952 marked the dawning of a new Elizabethan Age when Princess Elizabeth became Queen and reigning sovereign of the United Kingdom and of the British Commonwealth and Empire. The following year saw the nation celebrating the coronation and the conquering of the world's highest mountain, Everest, by Sir Edmund Hillary and Sherpa Tensing as members of Colonel John Hunt's expedition. Rock'n'Roll, Teddy Boys and blue suede shoes were on the horizon and 'teenagers' were about to be invented!

Right: Six spirited Huddersfield lasses here, workers at the ICI plant on Leeds Road, who are clearly determined to enter into the celebratory mood of the day of the Royal visit. Did they make their own hats? These ladies are of an age to have spent much of their youth in wartime conditions, 'making do' was a way of life. There would have been no church bells to ring out at their weddings, the lack of 'nylons' didn't get them down, they simply substituted gravy browning to colour their legs and a lead pencil marked out a 'seam'! For the girls called up to work in the Ordinance Factories, working three full shifts meant permission to buy make-up, foundation, face powder and a lipstick after the fourth shift. The 'blackout' curtailed their social lives and they were used to the rationing of food. Along with the proverbial 'kitchen sink' these women would have carried the all important Ration Book in their handbags, still in use in 1949, the year this photograph was taken, and four years after the war had ended. Readers may remember asking Mums for a 'coupon' to buy sweets and may also remember how Mum had to think it through carefully before giving permission.

By the mid-1950s the ICI works in Huddersfield was the largest employer in the area with over 5,000 staff and hundreds of contractors based at the Leeds Road site.

Above: The red carpeted steps of the suitably adorned Town Hall are the backdrop to this photograph of civic dignitaries with Her Royal Highness the Princess Elizabeth in July, 1949. The Town Hall had been described as a 'Palace of Flowers'. The dining room, where the Royal Couple had lunch, had a principal colour scheme of pink and mauve created with roses and scabious. Mr FW Martin and his staff from Greenhead Park were complimented on the taste, imagination and flair shown in their floral designs and arrangements. The Princess is seen here chatting to the Mayor, Alderman DJ Cartwright, and beside him stands his daughter, the Lady Mayoress, Shirley Cartwright. At the very back of this shot, standing on the Town Hall steps, is Mr JPW Mallalieu MP, member for Huddersfield and, immediately in front of him, in the short wig, is the Town Clerk of the time, Mr Harry Bann. The Earl of Scarborough was on hand to make the initial introductions and the Recorder of Huddersfield, Mr HBH Hylton-Foster, also presented to the Royal Couple, can be seen in the longer wig.

The Duke of Edinburgh accompanied the Princess on this visit which formed part of a three day trip to the West Riding. Whilst the Princess stood on the Town Hall steps, the Duke inspected the Guard of Honour.

Alderman Cartwright, in his welcoming speech, said he had experienced difficulty in adequately expressing his heartfelt feelings about the presence of the Princess and the Duke and went on to say, 'Huddersfield is indeed highly honoured by your gracious visit, and as Mayor I am privileged to convey to both of you from all your people, a hearty Huddersfield welcome'.

Above: The Royal Daimler comes to a halt outside the Town Hall and the Royal Couple prepare to greet the people of Huddersfield. In this photograph, Princess Elizabeth is seen shaking hands with the Lady Mayoress, Shirley Cartwright, who is standing beside her father the Mayor, Alderman Cartwright.

At the bottom left of this shot, members of the WRAC can be seen standing smartly to attention and behind them a section of wildly cheering, flag waving and densely packed crowd. Barriers had been set up in Ramsden Street, opposite the Town Hall, to create space for the Royal motorcade and for the 100 soldiers forming the Guard of Honour to form up. Nowadays, the sound of military boots marching and the sight of rifled soldiers being drilled is, to the average civilian, not much more than pure pomp and circumstance. To the people of Huddersfield watching this occasion in 1949 with their memories of the war still fresh, it must have been an evocative and stirring sight. Memories of wartime deprivations, the joy of VE Day and memories of the sorrow and sadness for those who would never come back. The presence of the WRAC acts as a reminder of the roles played by the women of Huddersfield during the war. Women replaced men in factories, engineering and armaments, they worked the land as part of the Land Army and, of course, they 'joined up' and served as drivers, nurses, plotters for the RAF and in many other ways.

Right: Her Royal Highness Princess Elizabeth soon after arriving at the Town Hall and carrying her bouquet of pink carnations and green ferns which had been presented by the Lady Mayoress. In this shot, with Prince Philip behind her, she is seen shaking hands with Colonel Laurence. The Mayor and Mayoress are on the left of the picture and Mr JPW Mallelieu, MP for Huddersfield, is behind the Mayor. The Earl of Scarborough performed the initial introductions. Luncheon was taken in the Town Hall, the Princess accompanied by the Mayor and the Duke by his daughter, the Lady Mayoress. A loyal toast opened the proceedings followed by a toast to the Royal Couple. The Mayor then presented a set of records of the world renowned Huddersfield Choral Society singing Handel's Messiah. The Choral Society had quietly taken their places in the room during the toasts and, immediately the presentation ended, gave a reportedly thrilling and spine-tingling rendition of the National Anthem. The Princess and the Duke were obviously impressed by the singing and Mr Mallelieu said that it was the most impressive performance of 'The King' that he had ever heard. Mr Herbert Bardgett, chorus master, was presented to the royal visitors before they left and was asked where the singers came from and did they ever visit London?

The Duke was amused when Mr Bardgett told him that a girl of 18 might have to wait until she was 24 to gain a place in the Society. The Princess and the Duke clearly very much appreciated the quality of the singing they had heard and kept Mr Bardgett in conversation for a full five minutes.

The Mayor also expressed a hope that, in the fullness of time, when the Baby Prince listened to the records he would be 'stimulated with a desire to visit our town and our people.' The Baby Prince was of course, Prince Charles, Prince of Wales, who was eight months old at the time.

These ladies knew the way to a man's heart was through his stomach! The girls from the ICI canteen on Leeds Road prepare to celebrate the visit of Princess Elizabeth and Prince Philip in July, 1949. Are you here? Do you know anyone here? The peep-toed shoes of the lady on the left edge of this shot will stir memories in many a female reader's heart - we just had to have a pair! The flag proudly unfurled by the dark-haired woman at the front of the shot appears to be the Red Ensign, the flag of the Merchant Navy, and known fondly as the 'red duster'.

Crowds lined the route of the Royal motorcade as it made its way along Leeds Road to the football stadium where the children of Huddersfield were to have their moment with the Princess and the Duke. A guard of honour made up of 120 representatives of Huddersfield youth organisations stood at the entrance to the stadium and a white flag hoisted from the Directors Box signalled that the Royal couple had taken their seats. Thundering cheers greeted the flag from the 8,000 children in the stadium, grown-ups had to stand outside perched on the roofs of nearby factories or on the slopes surrounding the ground to catch a glimpse of what was going on. Representing the teachers of Huddersfield, Miss EK Sykes, was presented to the Princess and the Duke as were the Director of Education, Mr H Kay and the chairman of the town football club, Mr Haydn Battye. The children sung out a rousing national anthem and then gave a display culminating in a tableau forming the letters E and P in blue, brown and pink. They then proceeded to mob the royal car as it attempted to leave the stadium, the police eventually clearing a path to allow the car to move forward.

Above: A charming and very natural shot of Her Royal Highness the Princess Elizabeth on a visit to Huddersfield in July, 1949. The Princess, on a three day visit to the West Riding, was accompanied by her husband, the Duke of Edinburgh - unfortunately blocked from our view on this shot by the Princess's becoming and stylish hat! The Huddersfield Daily Examiner of the day reported murmurs of admiration from the thousands watching the Princess as she stood outside the Town Hall chatting to the Mayor. Lime green and white were her chosen colours for the simple taffeta dress she wore. As can be seen in this photograph, the fabric had a tiny check and the dress was full-skirted with three-quarter length sleeves and pleated detail at the neckline. White elbow length gloves with matching handbag and ankle strapped shoes gave typically royal chic to the outfit. Her hat was of natural straw with small white flowers and lime green bows decorating the outer brim and a matching bow of lime green velvet inside the brim. Diamonds and pearls completed Princess Elizabeth's outfit, a three-string necklace with diamond clasp and a small diamond brooch shaped like a flower. The Lady Mayoress wore a powder blue dress trimmed with white broderie-Anglais edging around the shawl collar and a matching white hat.

This exceptionally natural and charming shot was taken as the Princess was about to leave Learoyd's Mill by Peter Eastwood who was, at that time, working as an apprentice for Mr Morris Bray the photographer.

Top: A relaxed future Queen Elizabeth with the Duke of Edinburgh to the left of the shot, is seen here shaking hands with Mr E Overton of Learoyd Bros of Trafalgar Mills on Leeds Road. The Lady Mayoress, Shirley Cartwright, is seen to the right of the Princess. Note the upper right hand corner of this photograph where workers in overalls can be seen balancing on roofs and ledges to try and get a view of the Royal Couple. Although serious faced police officers surround the Princess and her husband, the closeness of the crowd can be glimpsed to the right of centre of this picture between the Princess and the police officer and at the right hand edge of the shot. Security there was but not of the 1990s variety!

The trip to Learoyd Bros worsted mill was almost the last port of call on this 1949 visit to Huddersfield and Their Royal Highnesses were given an enthusiastic and 'right royal' welcome by the staff. The attractive, ivy-covered Trafalgar Mill building had been specially decorated inside and the workers were delighted at the interest the Royal Couple showed in the various procedures involved in producing cloth. The fine worsted cloth for which Huddersfield had achieved world wide fame.

Below right: The crowds, the photographers, the bunting, the sounds of military boots and commands, the excitement and party mood are conveyed well in this shot of the Duke of Edinburgh inspecting the Guard of Honour outside the Town Hall in Ramsden Street. It's a sunny and warm Tuesday afternoon in July, 1949 and our future Queen and her husband are paying an official visit to Huddersfield. The bare-headed Duke can be seen slightly below centre of the shot and in the crowd to his left, an excited lady in a light coloured outfit and dark hat is desperately trying to attract his attention.

The Guard of Honour was made up of representatives of 538 LAA Regiment RA, 578 HAA Regiment RA (5th Duke of Wellingtons), and the 7th Battalion Duke of Wellingtons. The Duke, accompanied by Colonel Laurence, stopped and chatted with Colour-Sergeant George Radcliffe of Slaithewaite, Lance-Bombadier Herbert Barker of Sheepridge and Sergeant Arthur Cotton of Edgerton. Perhaps they exchanged a few words about wartime service or medal ribbons adorning the uniforms of these brave men.

This being a visit to Yorkshire, cricket must feature somewhere and it did on this Royal day. The Duke had earlier in the day received a telegram from Mr Herbert Robinson, President of the Huddersfield and District Cricket League, which read, '10,000 members of the Huddersfield Cricket League extend to you, the President of the MCC, and to Her Royal Highness Princess Elizabeth their loyal greetings'. Mr Robinson received a telegram in reply that same afternoon. It read, 'Please extend to all members of Huddersfield Cricket League our grateful thanks for your kind message. PHILIP.'

Below: Duraglit for badges and buttons, blanco for belts and spit and polish for boots were the orders of the day here as officers inspect the soldiers selected for the Royal Guard of Honour. This is the parade ground of St Pauls Street Drill Hall where the guard formed up before marching into place outside the Town Hall. Black leather toecaps turned into patent glass mirrors after the application of a layer of black boot polish, applied quite thickly with the first two fingers in a duster or rag. Spitting on to the polish came next followed by serious rubbing of the area again with the first two fingers in soft rag or duster using small circular movements. Younger readers may care to try it on their Doc Martins!

Cheering multitudes of Huddersfield people let their hair down at the first Royal visit since the war and the happiest Huddersfield scenes for many years greeted Princess Elizabeth and Prince Philip on their visit to the town in July, 1949.

The Mayor tried hard to make himself heard above the crowd but it took several attempts before he could call for 'three cheers' for the Royal visitors. The response was reportedly deafening. To make sure of a good view of the event, several Huddersfield folk spent the night camped out on Ramsden Street, in front of the Town Hall and shared blankets during the cold small hours. The day dawned to grey skies in contrast to the brilliant and vibrantly coloured decorations but, by midday, the sun was shining on a warm and pleasant afternoon. At noon the military band struck up, adding more colour to the scene in their red uniforms, and the music caused a hushing of the murmuring crowd of thousands. Excited chatter broke out again as 12.15 chimed and renewed enthusiasm fluttered around the crowd as they realised that the Royal party were about to arrive. The guard commander brought his two ranks smartly to 'shoulder arms'. Not a muscle twitched on the serious intent faces of the soldiers. Two booming beats on the big drum halted the music. A hush descended for a second as the Chief Constable's car came into view and then deafening cheering and greetings as the Princess's standard flying from the royal Daimler was spotted by the crowd. The band struck up again, this time playing the National Anthem as the Princess stepped from the car at the red-carpeted steps of the Town Hall.

A charming and endearing shot of children from the Waverley School waiting in the warm sunshine of a Tuesday afternoon in July, 1949. The children are waiting patiently in excited anticipation of seeing the Royal Couple, Her Royal Highness the Princess Elizabeth and the Duke of Edinburgh, as they arrive in Huddersfield by car for an official visit to the town. Can readers recognise anyone here? Even the little ones in the very front row will be in their fifties now! The hairstyles worn by the little girls evoke memories of partings and hair held back by 'clips' or 'Kirbygrips', not in vogue these days. One or two plaits or pigtails can be seen and female readers may recall the pleasures of long hair being thoroughly brushed, pulled and tugged into tight plaits and then tied with a ribbon by loving Mums - whilst they wriggled and complained!

The girls of the Waverley School are seen here in their neat, mauve, uniform dresses. The youngest girls are carrying posies of red, white and blue flowers whilst the older ones wave flags. Only a handful of boys in this picture but they do the male of the species proud with their shining, neatly combed hair and ties. Where are they now?

The traditional Longwood Sing on Thump Sunday in September 1953. The Maple Leaf Four had been starring at the Palace the year before but who had the most fun, these singers or that audience?

The Sing is held each year on Thump Sunday which was originally the second Sunday in August but is now the first Sunday in September. The venue is Nab End Tower in Longwood which was erected in 1860-61 reputedly by unemployed men 'to give them an occupation'. Whether this means that the men decided to build a tower rather than be idle or whether someone gave them instructions to build a tower is unknown. The view from the top of the tower will extend for miles across the valley and could have provided some kind of inspiration or motivation for the building. The tower stands 23 feet above the flat surface of the quarry which is the location for the Sing, and has a diameter of 110 feet. Inside its walls are 24 steps leading to the top. The first Sing was held in 1873 and began at 7 am. Hymns and 'choruses' were the repertoire for this traditional local event. The inscription on the wall at the back of this photograph, upper left, could refer to the date of the first ever Longwood Sing described as 'the Mother of all Sings'. By 1959 a total of 89 'sings' had been held and money collected and given to charity.

Above: An aerial view of things! A very popular attraction at the ICI Children's Gala in June 1960, was to be taken for a ride in the works Simon Platform - suitably caged of course! By the mid-fifties ICI had become Huddersfield's biggest employer with over 5,000 staff and hundreds of contractors working out of the Leeds Road Site.

How many children would have to be catered for at this annual gala day event? How many children would have received ice-creams and presents at the ICI Children's Treat held at the ABC? Rather a lot!

1960 was the year in which, Huddersfield lad, Harold Wilson first challenged for leadership of the Labour Party. He failed to defeat Hugh Gaitskill in that year but took over as leader after Mr Gaitskill died in 1963. Mr Wilson always thought of himself as a 'Huddersfield man' although he moved to the Wirral in Cheshire when he was 16. Born on March 11th, 1916 on Warneford Road, Cowlersley, the family moved a year later to nearby Western Road. The young Harold attended New Street Council School in Milnsbridge and then Royds Hall Grammar School in Paddock. He became a labour MP in 1945 and was Prime Minister from 1964-70. Later he became Lord Wilson of Rievaulx.

Other famous Huddersfield faces include James Mason the Hollywood film star, Derek Ibbotson the world record breaking athlete, Anita Lonsborough Olympic Swimming Champion, Gorden Kaye the actor of 'Allo 'Allo' fame, the late Roy Castle and, perhaps not known by some readers, Patrick Stewart who found fame as Captain Jean-Luc Picard in Star Trek was born in Mirfield.

Top: Well slap my thigh! It must be Robin Hood and Maid Marion and all the Merry Men in Sherwood Forest. Oh no it isn't! Oh yes it is! This photograph shows the ladies of Meltham Church in action in December 1956. Nothing could be more traditional than a Christmas pantomime - unless it was a trip to the circus.

The circus has been a regular visitor to Huddersfield with both Bertram Mills and Billy Smart putting on shows. Are any readers prepared to own up to the fact that they can remember seeing the circus elephants parade from the railway station to Greenhead Park? In June 1953, coronation year, Billy Smarts Circus placed an advertisement in the Examiner for their 'Coronation Programme'. The 1,000 unreserved seats were priced at 2/- to 10s 6d - 10p to 52p - and reserved seats would knock you back 4/- to 10s 6d - 20p to 52p. Exorbitant! The main attraction was the arrival of the elephants at Huddersfield railway station at 3 pm on Sunday, June 14th and the subsequent parade through the streets to Greenhead Park.

Do readers know of the Hollywood connection with Huddersfield? Holmfirth in old English is 'Holne Frith' which means 'Holly Wood' and, had it not been for the First World War, Holmfirth could quite easily have become the Hollywood of England. The Bamforth family of Holmfirth were pioneers of 'moving pictures' and were also very successful. Their work was mostly comedy featuring local characters and was screened as far away as Russia. The Great War brought an end to film production and the family found great success in the production of saucy seaside postcards. The ladies of Meltham Church therefore, came within around fifty years of being film stars!

Below right: Huddersfield is honoured indeed! The re-opening event of the Huddersfield Co-op was important enough to attract the attentions of the lady herself - Mrs Annie Walker, (actress Doris Speed), landlady of the Rovers Return on Coronation Street. Beside Annie is husband Jack Walker, the landlord of the Rovers, who would have to jump to it when Annie called 'Jack' in that certain, two syllabled way invariably accompanied by a pursing of the lips and outraged movement of the head and shoulders. Another famous Jack is in charge of the Rovers nowadays, Jack Duckworth, together with another famous landlady, Vera Duckworth. The series depicting northern life, albeit from the wrong side of the Pennines, has been running for 40 years and is as popular today as it was when this photograph was taken - November, 1963.
Annie Walker was always 'dressed up to the nines' as the saying went, with make-up, not a blonde hair out of place and usually a several stranded necklace. In this shot the real life Doris Speed is wearing fur. Acceptable even admired in 1963 but totally out of order in the politically correct 1990s after campaigning by, amongst others, the 'supermodels'. An advertisement in the Huddersfield Examiner of October 1973 was headed 'Spotlight on Fur'. Nowadays that headline would be followed by an article about minks being freed by a pressure group or some well known person spelling out the case for the preservation and well-being of furry animals. In 1973 there followed advertising for Maxwell Cowan of Cloth Hall Street and a list of fur garments available for sale, a mink jacket at £245 or a Marmot coat for £95. A mink coat used to be the traditional gift a wealthy man would make to his wife, a symbol of success. Wearing one would be an embarrassment now!

Bottom: It is the swinging 60s, it is party time but no-one on this shot seems to be smiling. Perhaps the bar hadn't opened on time! This is the ICI Works Ball in March, 1962 held at the Huddersfield Town Hall. This photograph

illustrates the changes in dancing fashion which came in with the Rock and Roll era. Some couples in this shot can be seen to be jiving or attempting to jive on the crowded dance floor. A couple to the right of the shot, the lady is wearing a pale coloured outfit, appear to be dancing in the current fashion, ie independent of each other. Were they moving to an early Beatles number - 'Love Me Do'? Could Bill Haley and the Comets have tempted them to take up turpsichore with 'Rock around the Clock'? Were they enjoying the rhythm of a Lonnie Donegan's skiffle band and 'My Old Man's a Dustman'? Remember skiffle bands? Everyone could have one! All you needed was a rubbing board and thimbles, an old tea chest, a broom handle and a long piece of string. The long piece of string was attached to the broom handle like a string on a cello, the broom handle was inserted into the middle of the tea chest and the 'instrument' was played by 'twanging' the string. The rubbing board and thimbles needs no explanation unless you are too young to know what a rubbing board was. Ask your Mum!

The judging of the Fancy Dress Competition at the ICI Children's Gala in June 1962 and who could pick a winner from this excellent selection. It was so much more fun in the days when everyone made their own costumes rather than rent them from a specialist shop. Miss Quality Street looks most attractive as does the Japanese girl, Charlie Chaplin is further down the line with, is it, Night and Day looking up at a judge? Yogi Bear towards the end of the line, right hand edge of the shot, was a popular cartoon character and catch-phrases involving 'Boo-boo', Yogi's sidekick were on everyone's lips. The little girl on the left hand edge of the shot is wearing what many little girl's of the period would have wanted from Santa - a nurses outfit. Is the pretty little girl wearing headgear tied with a ribbon dressed as a strawberry? What imaginative costumes had been made from household items.

The sixties was the decade of the 'Drinka Pinta Milka a day' slogan, John Wayne was starring at local cinemas in 'The Commancheros', local garages held such classics as the Austin Healey Sprite and the Austin A40 and Newton's filling station still stood on Viaduct Street. Boyes Garage had marques such as Standard, Morris and Singer for sale and, in 1966, the newly launched Triumph 1300 could have been yours for £796 12s 11d - work that one out in new pence!

Above: 'Bringing out the Colours' in 1948, are the 7th Duke of Wellingtons Regiment. The gentlemen marching in civilian clothes are likely to be veterans of the Great War. The 'Dukes' have the right to march through the streets of Huddersfield with colours flying, bayonets fixed and bands playing on all ceremonial occasions after being granted Freedom of the Borough after the Second World War. The Dukes have a long history with the West Riding and, since 1782, most soldiers have been recruited from this area which explains the feeling of the Dukes being 'our' regiment. Arthur Wellesley, later the first Duke of Wellington, held positions of command with the regiment between 1793-1802 and 1806-1813 but it wasn't until after his death in 1852 at the age of 83 that the regiment's request was fulfilled and they became known as the Duke of Wellington's Regiment.

Previously known as the 33rd (or 1st Yorkshire West Riding) Regiment, the men of the regiment met up again with their former Colonel at the Battle of Waterloo in 1815. This is the battle which will be forever associated with the Dukes and took place over the day of June 18th, Trafalgar Day. A frustrated Napoleon Bonaparte is reported to have said, 'These dogs of English never know when they are beaten'. That was probably because they weren't beaten! Forty years of peace followed to be broken by the Crimean War in 1854. The Dukes have been involved in all major world conflicts from the American War of Independence through to recent hostilities in the Balkans and have been awarded 117 Battle Honours. Descendants of the first Duke have maintained close links with the regiment - the only British regiment to be named after a commoner - and the 8th Duke is currently Colonel-in-Chief of the regiment. A small regimental headquarters is maintained at Wellesley Barracks in Halifax and the Regimental Museum is at Bankfield Museum in Halifax. The regiment will celebrate its 300th anniversary in 2002.

Below: Huddersfield is known world wide as a town which produces fine worsteds. Fine cloth makes fine clothes and the staff of George Hall, the fashion store, take to the catwalk here to model the garments for sale in the store. The audience is made up of members of the general public who don't look particularly impressed but Huddersfield lasses have always had their feet on the ground and have never had their heads turned easily by fancy ideas. The date of this photograph is April 1959 and the clothing being modelled is the new Spring range.

World War II brought fashion to a halt with both sexes wearing trousers and clothing having of necessity to be practical and makeshift. In the early 1950s readers may remember Norman Hartnell's 'New Look' favoured by the Royals and often associated with Princess Margaret. The 'New Look' had almost ankle length, full skirted garments with nipped in waists, high heeled shoes and small hats. A popular and sought after garment was a navy grosgrain coat with a narrow shawl collar. Men favoured an Edwardian look with exaggerated, wide shoulders and 'Teddy Boys' arrived on the scene with sideburns, as they were known in America, or 'sideboards' as they were commonly called here. By the late 1950s womens clothes had returned to the straight lines of the 1920s and 'bouffant' hairdos, with oceans of hair lacquer were all the rage.

Do you remember buying 'Miner's' hair lacquer in a glass bottle and pouring it into a plastic spray bottle? Young men began to wear clothing resembling that of motor-bikers, such as black leather jackets, in the rebellious early 1960s and began to wear their hair very long and often with a fringe. Denim jeans became popular and were worn as much by young women as young men. Both sexes wearing similar clothing and both sexes adopting long hair made this the decade of 'unisex'. In other words, we all had trouble figuring out if the figure in the distance was a man or a woman!

Look carefully at this photograph! Are you sure you don't recognise anyone present? It is the ICI Children's Gala in June 1959 and the crowd appear to be rapt in attention. They were watching the fancy dress competition.

These youngsters will be middle aged now, it's interesting to ponder on what their lives might have held in contrast to the lives of their parents. These young lads wouldn't have been 'called up' to fight in a devastating war and face up to the loss of life and limb. These young girls wouldn't have to say goodbye to husbands, sons and brothers not knowing if they would ever see them again. The parents of these youngsters would be heartily thankful for that. These children had the benefits of the National Health Service, of access to better education and university places. They saw television come into everyone's home and they could hope for a much higher standard of living as technology advanced at a rapid rate. But, by the time they themselves became parents, did their children have as much fun? Does the modern trend towards electronically produced entertainment, videos, Nintendos, computer games, provide the fun, laughter, camaraderie and friendship which used to be found at group events such as the one shown here? Are we too sophisticated for this kind of event in the 1990s or do we just think we are?

A winning entry here in the fancy dress competition at the ICI Children's Gala in June 1959 - and deservedly so! What an imaginative costume and what effort and ingenuity has gone into its, no doubt, home made creation. In case it's just on the edge of your memory and driving you to distraction:-
' There was an old woman who lived in a shoe, she had so many children she didn't know what to do, so she gave them some broth without any bread, then whipped them all soundly and sent them to bed.'

Prizes on the table include a compendium of games which includes tiddly-winks, snakes and ladders and draughts. You must have had a compendium of games as a gift some time! Perhaps delivered by Santa? How long is it since you've played a game of Snakes and Ladders?
A sunny and warm summer afternoon - but weren't they always then? The compere's microphone can be seen to the left of the shot, beside the man in the white shirt. They don't look like that any more do they?

tiny house, In a tiny house, By a tiny stream, By a tiny stream, Lived a lovely lass, Lived a lovely lass, with a lovely dream, with a lovely dream, and the dream came true, and the dream came true (all together now) quite unexpectedly in Gilly gilly horse and pepper castenella vogen by the sea -ee-ee!

Top: Rawthorpe Children's Field Day in June 1953 and the Fancy Dress Parade stopped the traffic! The scarecrow in the foreground is giving an Oscar winning performance and to his right we have Mary, Mary Quite Contrary and Little Red Riding Hood. Old Mother Hubbard stands behind 'Contrary Mary' and Aladdin, Robin Hood and a very fierce looking pirate are all present. Towards the back of the group a chimney sweep can be spotted with his brush poking above the heads of the other children.

This, of course, is a fancy dress parade, but nevertheless the sight of the sweep's brush recalls the days of coal fires and the dreaded sight of a fall of soot on the hearth one morning indicating a visit from the chimney sweep was called for. Sheets would be spread to protect the carpet and the furniture and the hearth rug rolled up and moved out of the way. Someone would have to run outside to look for the brush poking out of the top of the chimney to make sure it had gone all the way up! The Austin parked at the left hand edge of the shot is a police car, no flashing blue lights or colourful stripes in 1953 when the level and nature of crime was generally lower and much different today. This Rawthorpe event was clearly very popular and well attended as is evidenced by the crowds approaching down the road, back centre of the shot, and the people coming out their homes to watch the parade.

Above: Everyone must remember the old song sheets at the pantomime! One of the players would have a stick to point out the words and absolutely everyone joined in. One side of the auditorium would be challenged to sing louder than the other and the girls would attempt to shout down the boys. This was all arranged so that the cast could have a few minutes respite from the physical rigours of pantomime and an opportunity to change and dress for the finale. These children could be receiving sweets as prizes or beans to grow a beanstalk like Jack's. Whatever the case, they are enjoying themselves especially the little girl at the far right of the picture.

This photograph was taken in January, 1952 and shows children on the stage of the Palace Theatre in Huddersfield enjoying the annual treat organised for the children of workers at the ICI plant on Leeds Road. A favourite pantomime song for communal singing was 'In a Tiny House', and it went something like this:- In a

Above: The date is May 1953, the venue is Huddersfield Town Hall and the event is Speech Day for Central (Kayes) College. A well turned out group of young people deserving the maximum attendance from parents and guests evident in this photograph. The Mayor and Lady Mayoress are present at the prizegiving table and it appears, from the stance of the people in the audience, that the national anthem is being sung. The Town Hall was a regular venue for secondary and grammar school Speech Days. The late 1950s to early 1960s saw the opening of many new secondary schools in Huddersfield and in November 1958, Her Royal Highness the Princess Margaret came to Huddersfield to open the Salendine Nook Schools site.

Anyone who can remember being at school in the fifties will also remember 'school milk' and the national outcry when it was abolished. Every child was given a third of a pint of milk in a small, specially sized milk bottle and a straw to drink it through. Those crates of tiny milk bottles were such a familiar sight on school premises! People born in the war years, 1939-45, will all remember school milk and will also have been raised through the years of food rationing which didn't end until 1950. Those people are now in their mid to late fifties and their numbers include people such as Sir Cliff Richard. Perhaps there was a rejuvenating quality to rationed food and school milk!

Above: It has been said that all of Huddersfield's social set, the people who attended functions in and around Huddersfield in the 1950s and 60s, would know the gentleman on this photograph. He is the late Mr Harry Ogden known as 'Flash Harry' and night after night throughout the season he would be in charge of the bar at one event or another.

He appears to be in charge of three charming ladies here and a great many empty glasses. The four of them couldn't possibly be responsible for emptying all of them could they?

Above: A love of music and in particular choral singing are deep rooted traditions in Huddersfield and the Huddersfield Choral Society has achieved worldwide fame. Some of the many local amateur instrumental and choral groups have also made recordings. This photograph shows The Huddersfield Choral Society performing in the concert hall of the Town Hall for a BBC concert in May 1968. The vast organ, seen at the back of the shot, is named 'Father Willis' and is used for lunchtime organ recitals.

Seven years earlier, in October 1961, Sir Malcolm Sergeant had been awarded Freeman of the Borough of Huddersfield for his 'unparalleled service to music'. The award was presented by the Mayor of the time, Alderman HF Brook, and the President of the Huddersfield Choral Society, Mr GDA Heywood. Sir Malcolm conducted the Choral Society in a performance of the Messiah in December 1961.

The Choral Society performed for royal visitors in 1949 when they sang the national anthem for Princess Elizabeth and the Duke of Edinburgh during a royal visit. The Royal Couple, extremely impressed by the quality of the singing, were delighted to be presented with a set of Choral Society recordings and Mr Bardgett, chorus master at the time, told the Duke of Edinburgh that a girl of 18 wanting to join the Society would probably be 24 before she was given a place!

Huddersfield University is part of the town's musical tradition too having one of the largest music departments in the country and annually hosting the Huddersfield Festival of Contemporary Music.

Top: An audition for the next James Bond film or the Colne Valley Male Voice Choir? 'Father Willis' the impressive organ in the background, places this photograph, taken in May 1966, in the concert hall of Huddersfield Town Hall so it must be the Colne Valley Choir and not a group of Sean Connery look alikes!

Choral singing is a deeply rooted tradition in Huddersfield and many local, amateur groups have made recordings. The Huddersfield Choral Society is internationally renowned and has performed for and been conducted by, many famous and important guests. The Choral Society gives an annual performance of the 'Messiah' from this concert hall and, in 1961, they were conducted by Sir Malcolm Sergeant who had been given Freedom of the Borough.

Huddersfield's most famous musician is the late Roy Castle. A lad from Scholes, educated at Scholes Council School and Honley Grammar School, Roy was described by a critic as 'brilliant' whether he was singing, dancing or playing an instrument. Roy started to gain fame at the age of 15 and credited his parents with his early success. They forked out £100 for a drum kit for him - a small fortune in those days. He was at the top of the variety bill at the Ritz in Huddersfield in February 1959 shortly before leaving for the London Palladium - and the rest, as they say, is history!

Below: A much loved northern sound – the brass band. This photograph shows the well known Skelmanthorpe Silver Band as it was in 1960. The earliest documentation relating to a band in Skelmanthorpe dates back to 1843 and they are currently in the football equivalent of Division One of the 'bands league'. The Championship Section includes semi-professional bands such as Black Dyke Mills Band and the Brighouse and Rastrick. This section is followed by four others, one being the highest and next to the Championship Section and four being the lowest. The band has met with much success winning lots of awards including winning the National Third Section at Wembley in 1993. I you would like to hear them perform and what true northerner wouldn't, the Skelmanthorpe Band join forces with the Skelmanthorpe Male Voice Choir to put on a well attended concert at the Huddersfield Town Hall every October.

The name 'Skelmanthorpe' has interesting Viking origins. The name is likely to have originally meant 'the village of a man called Skialmar' or Skjaldmar'. Skialmar/Skjaldmar means a shield/a glorious Viking. However, as with all place names, corruption of pronunciation takes place over the years and the name Skelmir' the plural of which is Skelmar' meant a devil, a rascal or a rogue. The Viking word 'Skilmathr' meant a man of trust. So is Skelmanthorpe, in fact, the village of rogues and rascals or the village of men of trust? The latter of course!

Inset: Charm, elegance and grace - none of those are evident in this photograph! This shot shows some of the cast of the Longwood All Male Pantomime as performed in February, 1957. Over forty years ago, these young men will all be pensioners now, pensioners with happy memories of the pantomime. It looks very much as if a good time would have been had by all especially the make-up and costume department! It takes a lot of panstick to hide stubbly growth and tutus in delicate pastels and chiffon don't really go with knobbly knees and rugby player's calves!

The year after this photograph was taken, in 1958, headlines reported the Munich air disaster when eight players from Manchester United were amongst the 21 passengers killed and a wave of sympathy swept the country. The CND movement was born in the late fifties and Huddersfield still had trolley buses. World events which would have captured the interest of the people of Huddersfield included the commissioning of manned space flights in the USA, Christopher Cockerell perfected his hovercraft device which nowadays has transported millions of people across the channel. Charles de Gaulle became President of France and one of Britain's most popular and successful composers, Ralph Vaughan Williams, died at the age of 86.

Eleven pretty young women are all hoping to be Miss ICI Huddersfield in March 1962. The competition took place at the Works Ball which was held in the concert hall of the Town Hall. The venue can be identified by the presence of 'Father Willis', the magnificent Town Hall organ, in the background. The season, though not the month, could have been deduced by from the presence of daffodils and tulips in the splendid floral display in front of the girls. Bottom right of the shot is a large mirror lit with dressing table lights which shows us a lower section of the audience! Is that a pair of white stilettos on the feet of the lady in the front of the reflection? Were you there? The contestants' dresses are very much the fashion of the time and many were probably home made. Sewing and knitting the family's clothes was slowly being replaced by buying knitwear and other garments as mass production quickly made the latest styles available at prices the average citizen could afford. Ten years earlier every home would have had a 'rag bag' containing old garments, old curtains any kind of fabric which had

ceased to serve its usual purpose but which could be transformed into a frock or a pair of short trousers for a child. The announcement of a baby on the way led to everyone reaching for the knitting needles, swapping or borrowing patterns, the production of layettes, matinee jackets and lacy shawls for the new arrival. There would be discussion on which shade of pastel or traditional white should be used because, of course, no expectant Mum ever knew the gender of the baby she was carrying in those days. Fabric shops were plentiful and every market had its share of stalls selling material. The self-patterned brocade of the dress worn by contestant number one was a popular choice. Usually in shiny, pastel shades, powder blue or lilac was popular, the fabric had a flower or other motif woven into it or machine-embroidered onto it. The dark heavier pattern worn by the second girl, the checks worn by number 11 and the deeply coloured floral design on a white background chosen by the girl next to her will all strike a chord in readers memories - the ladies anyway!

Bottom: What memories are stirred up by the photograph here! It was taken in November 1963 at the re-opening event of the Huddersfield Co-operative Society's store on New Street after it had undergone extensive refurbishments.

Many readers will have owned, perhaps still own, light fittings exactly like the ones suspended from the ceiling of the Electrical Department shown here. The often cylindrical shades, usually three or four, made from opaque glass in colours from white to orange were often hung from a fashionably plain piece of wood, usually teak. For the bathroom it was always a glass globe which looked like a ping-pong ball often with a chrome rim which screwed directly onto the ceiling.

Centre of this shot, to the left of the saleslady, is a display of electric blankets. The Morphy Richards New Electric Under-blanket is on top of a pile of boxed Cozee-Comfort electric blankets. Remember how everyone worried about the condition of the wiring? We had to remember to turn them off before we got into bed or we risked being fried! Remember how cold cotton sheets could be in a bedroom without any form of heating in the winter?

In the bottom left hand corner of this shot are some 'coal effect' two bar electric fires. With the introduction of smokeless fuel and the general move away from domestic coal fires, many people bought fires exactly like these and stood them on the hearth on the tiled fireplace surrounds. To use both bars was extravagantly expensive but using one bar was never quite warm enough. Being warm is perhaps the greatest benefit we have gained in recent years.

Right: It is said that a log was kept by the technicians and maintenance crews at Emley Moor TV Station. It reputedly contained repetitious, monotonous entries such as 'nothing to report', 'nothing to report', 'nothing to report' day in, day out, week in, week out. Until one day in March 1969 when the long string of 'nothing to reports' was dramatically interrupted with an entry which read 'the mast fell down'! This photograph was taken looking from the TV station in the direction of the fall of the mast. In the top right hand corner of the shot Emley Moor Chapel can be seen with plastic sheeting over one corner of the building. This was the corner hit by the falling mast. The catastrophic failure of this structure also totally demolished a contractor's hut which was fortunately empty at the time. Had it happened an hour earlier people would have been injured, as things turned out there no injuries were sustained as a result of the mast collapsing.

As can be seen from this picture, the various parts of the mast had been given numbers by the investigating engineers who were trying to piece together the reasons for the mast's collapse. It took many weeks, a large team of workmen, three mobile cranes and several low loaders to clear the site.

Normal service was resumed as soon as possible!

A very classy do here and it's certain that they all came by car! It's possible that they all arrived in Jaguars or Armstrong Sideleys maybe even the odd Rolls Royce. These things are almost certain because this is the Huddersfield and District Motor Traders Annual Dinner in March, 1953. On the other hand the weather being what it was in March, 1953 - snow, snow and more snow - perhaps they'd had to arrived by horse drawn sleigh.

It would appear, from the evidence supplied in this photograph, that the ladies who wore fur jackets either kept them on or draped them over the back of their dining chairs. Many of the well dressed and stylish women at this dinner are in strapless or backless dresses or sleeveless and flimsy cocktail wear. The only women to be seen wearing outdoor clothing are those in fur jackets. The only jackets on the backs of chairs are fur jackets and wraps. Did everyone in humble tweed or woollen coats leave them in the cloakroom? Was it the status symbol of owning a fur that led to the fur clad ladies keeping their jackets on or draped over their chairs? A dramatic change in attitude regarding fur has taken place since this photograph was taken. Nowadays women would be proud of synthetic fur and not the real thing. How many of these women would have driven their husbands to the dinner? Not too many even though there was no breathaliser in 1953!

Great Oaks from little acorns

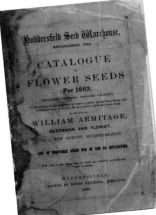

Real Peruvian guano was the thing to use on the land back in 1842, when William Armitage founded what was to become Armitage's Garden Centres. He had no way of knowing that his fledgling corn and seed warehouse would eventually become one of the oldest family-run businesses in the Huddersfield area.

William's background, however, was in a totally different field. After leaving school the young man had been placed with his uncles to learn the cloth milling business in Cawthorne, and eventually he and a friend went into business together as millers in Honley.

He was just 22 years old when, in 1830, he married Ann Bell, daughter of the landlord of the Golden Cross public house at Cawthorne. The enterprising young man set up shop as a seedsman, initially as a service to agriculture, in the Beast Market in Huddersfield. At last William Armitage had found something that he not only enjoyed doing but that quickly became a commercial success. After a few years he relocated to New Street, a prime site on one of the busiest streets in Huddersfield, where the business was to remain for more than a hundred years. The young couple were to have four children,

and their son Bell (who was given his mother's maiden name, an old Yorkshire tradition) joined his father in the business. Eventually the name Bell became traditional within the Armitage family.

Above left: The company catalogue, dated 1863.
Above right: The original shop with sacks of seeds being carted into the shop for sale to customers.
Below: Bell Armitage with sons, (from left to right) Bell, Charles, baby Tom and Edward circa 1875.

Once established at New Street, William Armitage's Corn and Seed Warehouse became renowned in the Huddersfield area. Agriculture and allotment gardening was very much a male domain back then - it was accepted that a woman's place was in the home, rearing the children, keeping the house clean and making sure there was a hot meal waiting for her husband when he came home from his place of work. A catalogue from 1862 still survives, and we can see this attitude reflected in the introduction, which begins 'Gentlemen...'.

Today's cookery and gardening programmes have made a number of

vegetables and herbs popular, which we have appropriated as 'modern' foods. Armitage's catalogue, however, opens our eyes to the fact that four different varieties of endive and an amazing thirty-seven varieties of herbs (with an aside that informs the customer that they have 'all other sorts of herbs' available!) were on offer. The ever-popular basil, marjoram, rosemary and thyme are on the list, but how many of our TV cooks use hyssop, scorzonera or marigold? Interestingly, capsicum and tomatoes (which, the catalogue explains, were also called love apples), are listed as herbs rather than as salad vegetables. When tomatoes were first gaining in popularity nobody seemed to know how to categorise them; a catalogue published a year later placed the 'love apple' seeds among the flowers.

At that time seeds were sold in Imperial measures as pints, half pints and quarts. Some varieties of early peas cost as little as sevenpence a quart, while French beans were much more expensive - scarlet runners were 1/6d a quart. Amazingly those old Imperial measures survive and are regarded by today's Armitage family as very much part of the firm's proud history.

William Armitage, who was born on 8th May 1808, died on his birthday, the 8th May 1876. He was 68 years old. His obituary perhaps gives us an insight into the reason for the success of the business he built up, informing us that he was 'upright and fair in all his dealings, scrupulously honest and tenacious of his word'. His son Bell was, of course, there to take over the running of the business. In turn his own sons Bell and Tom came into the firm; Bell's son - a third Bell, born in 1912 - also went on to join the firm.

The two world wars were difficult times for Armitages, and led to key changes where the employment of female shop workers were concerned.

Top left: William Armitage, the founder of Armitage & Sons **Left and right:** *Examples of two company catalogues, dated 1863, within the page at the top, it says 'Love apples' which are better known today as tomatoes and were once listed among the flowers.*

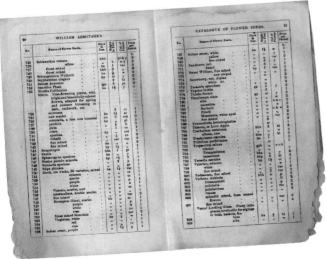

Before 1914 corn and seed was sold in two-hundred-weight bags, with ten bags to the ton. As some of the male workforce joined the military, however, women workers moved in to take over - and found the heavy bags rather hard to handle. The weight of the bags was therefore halved, making twenty bags to the ton. During World War II the nation was encouraged to 'dig for victory', and gardeners everywhere were replacing roses with potatoes and growing cabbages instead of lupins.

As the war went on, it was by no means certain that Armitage's warehouse would not take the full force of a bomb that would destroy the firm's entire stock of seed, and in 1941 Bell and Tom Armitage sent a letter to all established customers advising them not to delay purchasing their seed as 'no matter how much we were prepared to pay we could not replace them.' Fortunately Armitage & Sons, as the firm had become, survived the war unscathed and the company continued to prosper.

Above: One of the early examples of their company logo.
Top left: Bell and Vanda playing in the Armitage's delivery cart at Winter Garden Nurseries, Rowley Grove, Fenay Bridge, circa 1915/18.
Below: Tom Armitage with his children Vanda and Bell, circa 1915/18, at the Winter Garden Nurseries, Rowley Grove, Fenay Bridge.

By the early 1990s the garden machinery centre in Old Leeds Road was becoming too small for the firm's rapid expansion, and a nursery was discovered for sale in Birchencliffe. Though rather run down the place offered them exactly what they were looking for. It was demolished and rebuilt with a main emphasis on garden machinery, with an adjoining garden centre. With centres at each end of Huddersfield that were both easily accessible from the motorways, Armitages could at last offer their services to the entire Yorkshire area.

By 1963 The shop in New Street had become too small to hold the large amount of stock and equipment for which it had become noted. The company was now being headed up by Quinton and Alistair Armitage, great-great-grandsons of William, and the two young men began to look around for larger premises. Demonstrating the founder's enterprising spirit they moved to larger premises in Lord Street and took the opportunity to offer a range of garden furniture and a garden machinery sales and repair service, with a basement room acting as a workshop. Thirteen years later this side of the business expanded into premises on Old Leeds Road, which had a showroom as well as a workshop.

In 1985 the Pennine Garden Centre at Shelley came on the market; Armitages acquired the site, adopting the maxim 'town centre to garden centre'. Here there was plenty of space to spread out, so it was decided to vacate the Lord Street premises altogether and move that operation out to Shelley.

As has often been said, 'Great oaks from little acorns grow' - and over the last 155 or so years Armitages have amply demonstrated the truth of the old proverb. The extensive and impressive garden centres of today bear little resemblance to that first small business begun so long ago by William Armitage.

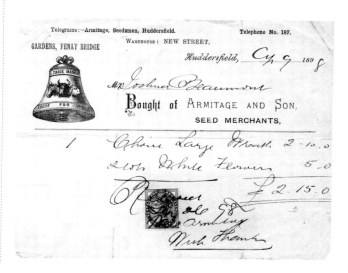

Above: *Bell, Fanny and Elizabeth Armitage in the grounds at the family home Rowley Grove, Fenay Bridge.*
Above right: *Tom Armitage, who was about twenty one at the time this photograph was taken.*
Right: *A reciept from Armitage & Sons dated September 1898, over one century old.*

The present William Armitage (Alistair's son) has taken over a key role within the company as Marketing Manager. William puts the firm's success down to a number of factors. The enthusiasm of the staff plays a key role; people can be taught how to do a job, but enthusiasm for the work is something which cannot be taught. Some of the company's long-serving employees have been with Armitage's since they left school. At Armitages the staff are encouraged to chat with customers, getting to know

them, finding out exactly what their requirements are - then meeting those expectations.

Alistair and Quinton, who are joint partners in the business, believe in being one hundred percent involved in the job. They are more likely to be seen stripping a mower down or assisting on the shop floor than sitting in an office. Other members of the family are also involved; Alistair's wife Diana is the gift and Christmas buyer for Pennine Garden Centre and Quinton's wife Val occupies the similar position at Birchencliffe.

At present, further developments are taking place within the Garden Centre at Birchencliffe as the machinery and the garden centre sales areas are expanded to give further space.

The company has expanded recently in ways that could not have been visualised even 20 years ago. Plants, for example, today form a major part of the garden centre, and the firm's incredible two-year guarantee on all hardy plants reflects their caring attitude towards their customers.

'We can't promise that a plant will grow for two years,' says William. 'That's up to the care it receives.' More often than not plants die because they are not looked after properly, and when a customer brings a dead plant back it gives us an opportunity to replace their plant and talk to them about plant care. The end result is that the customer will have a successful garden - and will return to Armitages again and again.

Nurseries from all over the UK and Holland deliver to the garden centres every week, bringing over customer orders and anything that looks good at that particular time. The company also imports from Australia and Italy and gardeners with a taste for the exotic often browse among the fascinating range of unusual plants on offer at Armitage's garden centres. Dicksonia, for example, was around 300 million years ago in the Cretaceous period, and is imported from Australia. But will it survive in chilly Huddersfield? customers want to know.

Left: As time goes by the shop looks bigger and better. This picture dates back to 1940s.

Plant Area Manager, John Mason's reply is that it certainly will, seeing that in its ancient past it survived meteor strikes, dinosaurs and global ice ages, and more recently in its Australian mountain home the plant regularly lives through thick snow and temperatures of minus ten degrees.

Garden furniture of all kinds including childrens' playhouses can be purchased in premises that turn out to be far more extensive than they look from the car parks. Indoors, customers can shop

for anything from a ride-on mower to a bag of daffodil bulbs. Children are thrilled by the pet departments at both centres while their parents can wander around the large book and gift departments. Most customers spend more time here than they

Above: *Huddersfield town centre busy with shoppers in New Street and on the right side of the photograph you can see Armitage & Sons with plenty of customers outside.*

Right: *Mr Alistair Armitage with a selection of seed catalogues in a picture dating from the early 1970s.*

anticipated, browsing among the gifts, planning their home and garden, then relaxing in the coffee shop with a wide selection of home made cakes and tasty snacks to choose from.

The first William Armitage would have much to be proud of, could he see what eventually became of his modest enterprise.

And what of the future?

The Armitage family would all agree that they intend to go on into the next millennium offering the same value for value that has always been the maxim of this highly successful Huddersfield company.

Today's career-minded men and women have little time for gardening so architectural plants and ready made gardens are very popular. A new house with a patio can be given an instant minimum care garden in pots which can be moved to new positions to ring the changes. Armitage's offer pots of every size that originate from all over the world - South America, the Mediterranean, Africa and Asia.

Above: *Sharpening mower blades in the workshop in the 1970s: Quinton on the left, Alistair on the right, with Hugh Stringer in the centre background.*
Below: *Armitages Mower World & Garden Centre at Birchencliffe, opened in the early 1990s.*

At leisure

All the fun of the fair at Hopkinsons Ltd Children's Gala in July 1959. Exide Double Life batteries appear to have donated the use of a loudspeaker van for announcing important events such as the sack race or the Mum's race - and the finding of straying tots! Everyone seen on this shot is very smartly and attractively dressed from the Dads in shirts and ties to the little girl in the pretty print dress on the zebra and the gleaming white shirt of the little boy on the giraffe. Where are they now? Approaching their fiftieth birthdays probably!

The outfit of the lady on the left of the shot was very fashionable at this time. Her dress could have been home made as many were in those days. The cotton fabric could have been bought by the yard - please note yard not metre! A yard was, (or is, dependant on your point of view), 36 inches. A metre is roughly equivalent to 39 inches, accurately a fraction more than 39 inches. The dress worn by the woman here would have taken around three yards of fabric to make and the skirt gathered before attaching to the bodice.

For dressmakers out there, the zip is particularly well fitted! The pattern of abstract roses on the fabric was a very popular one, the roses were often blue with green leaves on a white background. If you look carefully you will see that a fraction of lacy petticoat is showing below the hem of the dress. Petticoats were all important to ensure the skirt or dress 'stood out' sufficiently. This lady is also wearing seamed stockings! Remember wetting a fingertip or thumb to make sure your 'seams were straight'?

Below right: Could there have been a risk of things getting out of hand at the ICI Works Ball at Cambridge Road Baths in 1956? Could the gentleman in uniform to the right of the shot be a security guard? A former military man with knowledge of First Aid in case anyone took a drop too much or passed out from the heat? Are the attractive couple on stage singing a Connie Francis number? 'Where the Boys Are' perhaps? And what do the smartly dressed couple in the foreground have in that plastic sack?
The 'feel good factor' created by a happy evening out, music from a live band and wearing lovely clothes designed to be worn at special events.

Bottom: And a good time was had by all! This fancy occasion is the ICI Works Ball in January 1956 and the young couple in the foreground appear to be rebelliously trying out their jive technique amongst the more sedate couples in the background. Dances just aren't like this any more are they? Works Balls have been replaced by discos with deafening music which everyone tries to escape from - unless they're under thirty. Or the modern company Christmas 'do' might be lunch in a pub in your best office outfit. Dressing up ain't what it used to be! Look at the satin and taffeta in this shot, definitely evening wear. These women will have felt properly glamorous and looked totally different

from their daytime selves. They could also twist and twirl in high heeled shoes - how are their feet nowadays? The remnants of streamers can be seen under the feet of the dancers but there is no sign of a large silver many faceted ball hanging from the ceiling. Perhaps it was there but we just can't see it in this shot. What is for sure is that there would have been no laser or strobe lighting effects.

Haigh's Tours and we're ready to go. The back seat has been 'bagged' already, probably by high spirited young men who are intent on having a good time. This smiling group - are you there? - are probably, as it's August, setting off for the Huddersfield Holiday Week of 1953. Are they going to Blackpool? Could the destination be Scarborough or Bridlington? What is for certain is that they wouldn't have been travelling to Manchester to fly off to Spain or Greece or other Mediterranean resorts! They would have bought sticks of rock, a plate for grandma decorated with the name of the resort, 'a gift from Scarborough', and drunk Horlicks in cafes. The gentlemen in the group may have sent lewd and funny postcards to their workmates depicting colourful caricatures of landladies and scantily clad buxom girls on the beach. Would they have known that these same postcards had probably been manufactured by Bamforths in Holmfirth? Holiday Weeks were happy and exciting times to be long looked forward to and saved up for - it seems it was all too much for the little girl in front with the big bows in her hair. She is wearing a lovingly hand knitted 'bolero' style cardigan which was fashionable and popular at the time. Travelling by 'chara' as it was generally known, was the norm in the fifties. The word comes from the French 'char -a-banc' meaning literally, a horse-drawn carriage with benches, and only if you were really rather posh would you have said 'coach'! Huddersfield folk would have a day in Blackpool 'going on a chara trip'. This happy group are seen as they are about to depart from the bus station in August, 1953.

Above: This is how the ABC on Market Street looked after converting from one large into two small cinemas. A public house was also built and stood next door, to the right of this shot. It was called 'The Painted Wagon'. As can be clearly seen, Screen 1 was showing the 'X' rated 'Enter the Dragon' and Screen 2 would be showing 'Paper Moon'. Sadly all of this has now disappeared, demolished and replaced by a branch of Sainsbury's.

Once upon a time the old Ritz cinema showed films such as 'Ivanhoe' starring Robert Taylor, Joan Fontaine, Elizabeth Taylor and George Sanders, 'The Glass Mountain' with Michael Denison and Dulcie Gray. But films were never the only thing to watch at the ABC. Fashions shows, for example, were held there. In the late 1940s fashion shows were used a means of recruiting women into industry and, in Huddersfield, the girls who made the cloth displayed the cloth as an added encouragement to others. A young Huddersfield woman named Vera Falck, a mender employed by Learoyd Bros, was one of seven models who displayed dresses produced from cloth made in the West Riding in a fashion display named 'Concerning You'. The outfit Miss Falck wore had been designed in 1946 by Victor Steibel for a famous fashion magazine and was a suit, known as a 'costume' in those days, comprising a skirt and single breasted, fitted jacket. Miss Falck also featured on a display board for use in shops or showrooms under a slogan, 'A Learoyd Girl in a Learoyd Suiting. Suit by Jaqmar', and a very pretty picture she made.

Above right: A new style of cinema going. The ABC in Huddersfield, like many other cinemas in recent years, converted its 2,000 seat auditorium into two smaller units in February 1974 when the number of cinema-goers was tending to drop. Many people put the reduced numbers down to the high price of tickets others claimed that the new tendency to violence and shocking scenes made people turn away from the big screen. Whatever the real reason, the reduction in size and advent of the multi-screen cinemas has seen an increase in numbers 'going to the pictures'.

The popularity of a night out at the cinema can be illustrated no better than in Huddersfield. In the early fifties there were 20 town centre cinemas in business. How many can you remember? In August 1952 you could have chosen from the: Princess, Empire , Ritz, Curzon, Tudor, Picture House, Grand, Majestic, Lyceum, Savoy, Excelda, Regent, Carlton, Rialto, Plaza, Premier, Lounge, Regal, Waterloo, Cosy Nook and, in addition, The Winston at Slaithewaite, The Alhambra at Meltham, The Palace at Milnsbridge and the Ritz at Golcar. If you fancy a night out at the pictures these days there is only one cinema to go - the UCI near the McAlpine Stadium - but it does have nine screens.

A night out at the flicks! Or, in this case, an afternoon, a matinee, because these children are enjoying the free ice cream during the show at the ICI Children's Treat held at the Ritz in January 1957. Part of the Treat was always free ice cream during the show and a present when the show was over.

Perhaps the most striking feature of this photograph is that the man left of centre, handing out the tubs of ice cream, has a cigarette dangling from this mouth with around an inch of cigarette ash about to fall on something or someone. He is in a cinema, close to children and close to edible goodies - it just wouldn't happen these days. The usherette with the tray of ice cream held with a strap around her neck is an evocative sight indeed. This shot clearly shows the tiny lamp on the back of the tray which allowed the customers to see what was left. Members of the audience would rush to the front of the auditorium to try and beat the queue for ice cream. If you didn't you risked the choc ices being sold out or maybe all the 'drinks on a stick' ice lollies would have gone, the 'orange maids' tasted like fresh orange juice.

The greaseproofed cardboard tubs came with a small, wooden, flat spoon and it was heaven as the ice cream melted in the heat and the creamy liquid was left at the bottom! If you were lucky, strawberry flavour could have been on offer as well as vanilla and the chocolate on choc ices was definitely much much thicker!

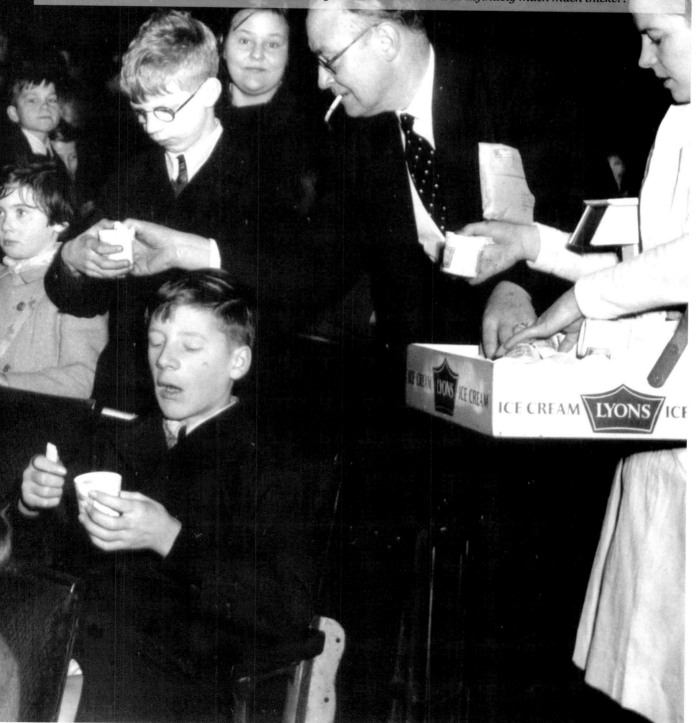

Is this a broadcast of 'Music while you Work'? Or it could be a broadcast of 'Workers Playtime'? Readers may remember the programme which often featured the comedian Arthur Askey. Vic Oliver was a popular radio musician. Sunday lunchtimes would see many a Huddersfield family gathered round the set to listen to 'Round the Horn' with Kenneth Horne. Mr George Tordoff remembers a joke from this show as, 'let me introduce this year's Miss Caterpillar. 'Ooh, she's got a nice pair of legs, pair of legs, pair of legs,......'. Mention of such radio shows as 'Dick Barton Special Agent' and 'Journey into Space' will evoke happy memories for many Huddersfield people. This is Huddersfield's Holme Moss TV transmitting station broadcasting music so it could it have been to accompany the famous potters wheel where the pot was never finished! Remember when there were on 'Intervals' on television? How many readers can remember Sylvia Peters and Mary Malcolm? They were announcers rather than presenters. Announcers popped up occasionally to describe the evenings viewing and were, in the early days, very well spoken young ladies immaculately coiffed and coutured who were greatly admired and very well known indeed. The Huddersfield Examiner reported in August 1952 that the BBC had decided to give Sylvia Peters and Mary Malcolm a whole new wardrobe. One of the gowns worn by Sylvia Peters was black guipure lace over green taffeta.

The Holme Moss TV station was built in May 1951, at the very dawn of the television age. Many people rented or bought sets for the coronation in 1953 and held 'open house' for their TV-less neighbours to come in and watch the event. Sandwiches were laid out on large dining tables so that no-one had to miss any part of the ceremony and those with tiny nine inch screen bought magnifiers, clear plastic screens which stood in front of the set. And the children watched Muffin the Mule!

Bird's eye view

A birds-eye view of pre-war Huddersfield taken in 1937. The lack of smoke from the forest of mill chimneys indicates that this could have been Huddersfield Holiday Week and therefore the month of August. The canal can be seen on the right of the shot curving around the mills which made Huddersfield wealthy and covered it in soot! A Ramsden, John, the 4th Baronet, saw the need for a canal in the town to improve communications with the outside world. The cost of £12,000 was met from his own pocket and John Ramsden hired the famous James Brindley to build his canal. It took six years to complete and in 1780 was connected up to the Calder at Cooper Bridge. The Huddersfield Narrow Canal linked Aspley Basin with Lancashire in 1811 and Huddersfield was placed well and truly on the map. The terraced homes of Huddersfield folk can be seen in this shot, bottom left and top right, although there was a drive in the 1920s and 30s to build housing estates outside the centre of town. This was made possible by the growing network of public transport which allowed people to live some distance away from their place of work. Many of the housing estates were built on the exposed hill-sides away from the industrialised Colne Valley. Some of these estates were located at Fartown, Sheepridge, Dalton, Birchencliffe and Newsome. Under a slum clearance plan older districts in the town were cleared.

Left: The ultimate challenge for 'Huddersfield spotters' is presented by this photograph dating back to May 1939. One or two pointers may be of help. If the ring road had been built, it would have curved across the bottom left hand corner of the shot. Market Street can be seen approximately half way up the left hand edge of the frame and it leads up to the large, pale coloured building of the Leeds Building Society. Left of the Leeds is Heywoods Department Store and beyond the Leeds and out of shot was the ABC cinema. The Plumbers Arms public house can spotted around one inch inside the upper left hand edge and High Street runs across the upper right hand side of the frame in front of the old soot blackened church. Albion Street runs centrally from the bottom edge of the picture into town with Cloth Hall Street becoming Buxton Road running alongside on the right. The patch of, what appears to be, white ground, upper left of centre, is now the location of the new Jobcentre and the Civic Centre is now to the right and nearer to the camera. May 1939 - how changed would the lives of the people of Huddersfield be over what was to come? The six years of World War II.
Below: A clear, sunny day and Trinity Street can be picked out running up from the bottom edge of this photograph,

slightly right of centre, with the New North Road to the left. Between the two lies what was the Royal Huddersfield Infirmary and is now part of the Technical College. The Princess Royal Hospital lies to the right of Trinity Street and in the bottom right hand corner of the shot.

Moving up the right hand side of the frame, the area of housing and trees is now the location of a car park and swathing across the shot from around the middle of the right hand edge towards the left hand corner is the new inner ring road. This photograph is taken from a north-westerly position. The most easily spotted landmark here is the railway station, middle left, with St Georges Square above it in the frame. Showing as not much more than a white speck on the roof of Lion Chambers is Huddersfield's famous big cat. The original 19th century lion was carved by John Seeley but has since been replaced by a fibre-glass model. Lion Chambers and Arcade were built between 1852-54 by Samuel Oldfield as an arcade of shops and warehouses. They stand on John William Street commemorating just one member of the Ramsden family who for so many years owned most of Huddersfield and played such an important role in the town's development.

> *The original Lion Chambers' cat (carved by John Seeley) has been replaced by a fibreglass model*

45

The month is June, the year is 1949 and the photograph is an aerial view of Huddersfield as it was almost fifty years ago. Had the inner ring road existed in 1949 it would have run across this shot from the bottom right hand corner area towards the centre of the top of the frame. The railway station shows up clearly at the lower edge of this picture with St Georges Square, the St George Hotel and, opposite, Britannia Buildings with the magnificent statue of Britannia on the roof. These buildings were the home of the Huddersfield Building Society and are now owned by the Yorkshire Building Society.

To the right of the station, New North Road runs in from the right hand edge meeting with Trinity Street which leads off to the upper right hand side of the frame. The area above Trinity Street is now car parking and, moving towards the top of the shot, the vent which extracts smoke from the railway can be seen standing as if it were on a modern-day roundabout. In the bottom left hand corner of the photograph, the Parish Church can be seen clearly and above it and a little to the right is the Market Place. New Street runs off towards the top of the picture with Market Street running to the right and almost parallel with New Street.

Three sections of underground heating were installed when the Ring Road was built

The familiar sight of the cooling towers and the power station provide perspective in this birds eye view of Huddersfield in August 1968. Lower centre of the shot, taken from the south-west, the Police Station, the Magistrates Courts and the Civic Centre, phase one, can be clearly seen. Chapel Hill runs up from the bottom right hand corner of the shot. Huddersfield motorists may remember poor road conditions during icy winters and plenty of skidding, slipping and sliding on Chapel Hill. Now a thing of the past since the installation of under surface heating on the steep approach gradient to the Chapel Hill junction with the inner ring road. Three sections of under surface heating were installed when the ring road was built, Chapel Hill as already mentioned, under the slip road from New North Road to the ring road and the approach and exit ramps of the underpass.

The Town Hall can be seen towards the right hand edge of this picture, just below centre. The railway station is upper left hand side with the George Hotel and Britannia Buildings visible to eagle eyed readers.

If you had been flying over Huddersfield in August 1968, this is what you would have seen. The bottom left hand corner of this shot shows Chapel Hill, from the bottom edge of the photograph, and Manchester Road, from the lower left hand side of the shot, converging at the roundabout.

Just above them the Police Station and Civic Centre can be made out. The area in the right hand corner of the frame is now the university and St Pauls church, now a concert hall, can be picked out as a landmark. To the left of the university area is now the site of the indoor market with the library discernible towards centre shot. To the left of the library, a little below centre, the Town Hall is outlined fairly clearly.

On the right hand edge of the shot at about the half way point, is Southgate and the Telephone Exchange. Crown House, the home of the Inland Revenue and the Benefits Agency, now occupies the area above the Exchange on this picture. Leeds Road can be seen curving away into the distance.

In 1978 six bottles of Webster's Green label would set you back 36p and a new bathroom suite could be had for £46.10

Huddersfield from the air in June, 1978 and some familiar sights here. Central to this shot is the Town Hall with library in view behind it. The new Market Hall can be seen to the right of the Town Hall. The spire of St Pauls Church pokes up clearly to the right and across the ring road from the Market Hall. The multi-storey car park is in front of the Market Hall in this shot, nearer to the camera. Chapel Hill leads into the frame to the Chapel Hill Roundabout, slightly below and left of centre, and behind the roundabout the Civic Centre, Magistrates Courts and the Police Station can all be seen. The building which appears to be Buxton House flats stands to the right of the Civic Centre in this photograph and somewhere near to it used to be the Mandarin Chinese Restaurant. A popular place to dine out for many Huddersfield people.

Five years before this photograph was taken you could have spent an evening at the ABC watching 'High Plains Drifter' and gone home afterwards for a cup of tea. You would have paid less than 8p for a 1/4lb of PG Tips. If you'd fancied something a little stronger, six bottles of Websters Green Label would have set you back 36p! You may as well have redone the bathroom - a new bathroom suite could be had for £46.10. On the other hand, if your job had been in a supermarket running a checkout a reasonable wage would have been £18 for a five day week - the bathroom suite doesn't sound as cheap now does it?

A line of Hanson's coaches, a familiar sight in Huddersfield, all waiting to transport children from the ICI Christmas Treat at the ABC Ritz Cinema in December 1958. The coaches were laid on to take children from outlying areas home safely. Children who lived nearer to the cinema can be seen in the foreground after being collected by Mum. Showing at the ABC is 'What Lola Wants' starring Tab Hunter. A 1990s mind on reading that film title would deem it unsuitable for children! However, the classification is shown as a 'U' which means it was considered suitable for a young audience. The classification 'A' was adults only and a category 'X' film indicated potential horror and/or terror or material which would be found tasteless by some - but possibly more innocent than programmes received on televisions in our living rooms these days. The present day system of film classification seems so very complicated by comparison. Is that the railway station building just in view, right hand edge of the shot, at the bottom of the street? There are definitely examples of the old 'Keep Left' signs on the small traffic island at the right hand edge of the picture. The old rubber 'sets' which used to pave the road outside the ABC have been replaced by tarmac by the time this photograph was taken. The rubber 'sets' were very slippery when wet and pedestrians, (and earlier, horses), often slipped and lost their balance in the rain. Trolley bus cables can be seen overhead and a fine example of an old belisha beacon on the left hand edge of the frame. Remember their bright orange glow?

Around the town centre

An excellent angle on St Peter's Parish Church on a sunny afternoon in June, 1969. St Peters was built in 1835-36 to replace an old church dating back to 1506 which had stood on the same site. The architect was the same Mr Pritchett who designed the railway station and he wanted to make maximum use of the old stone and flint from the original ancient building. He engaged a master builder who, although undoubtedly extremely skilled in his trade, was not a local man and it is said that the stone blocks were placed the wrong way round leaving the 'softer' side exposed to the elements and creating maintenance problems due to weather erosion ever since.

The Parish Churchyard, now St Peters Gardens, has a gruesome past. Between 1584 and 1850 over

38,000 bodies had been buried in the graveyard. It was so full that digging a new grave frequently meant disturbing an old and resulted in serious health risks and a dreadful stench!

The new Edgerton cemetery was therefore opened in 1850. In years gone by it had been the habit of the local weavers to display their 'pieces' of cloth by draping them over the wall of the cemetery.

However, the stench, and the uncertainties of the weather, led to the building of the Cloth Hall and some of the yards in the town centre.

This shot shows Lord Street leading off to the right and at its junction with Kirkgate. Readers may remember that buses for the Kirkburton side of the town used Lord Street as their terminus at this time.

As readers may have deduced from the fashions and the cars, this photograph was taken in the late 1950s, April, 1959 to be precise. This shot shows the junction of Market Street and Cloth Hall Street with Cloth Hall Street leading off to the right of the shot and we are looking down Market Street towards Westgate. The road in the foreground would at one time have been made of rubber sets to deaden the noise of passing traffic for the audience in the ABC cinema. Far left of this picture is Tetley's tobacco shop and next door resides Ken Lewell Electrical Ltd with its attractive and window-boxed facade. Woods Music shop now occupies these premises. The soot blackened corner premises are now the home of the Huddersfield Examiner offices and, further along, Crowther and Shaw are boldly advertising their stock of Kelvinator Refrigerators. To have a 'fridge in those days would have been rather posh! Readers may remember American films dating back to the fifties, black and white of course, and their depiction of the average American kitchen

equipped with 'fridge, space for table and chairs and fitted cupboards. Just a dream in those days! A cold slab in the larder would have been the most common way of keeping food cool. Crowther and Shaw subsequently moved to premises near to the bus station and have since moved again. GD Davies and Sons Ltd occupied the corner plot at the top of Cloth Hall Street and sold paint and household decorating products and equipment. Remember when gloss paint always dripped? Would anyone in 1959 have known what vinyl satin finish emulsion was? Dark green was a popular colour for the external doors and windows of Huddersfield homes in the fifties unlike today's bright white. Car buffs might be interested in the Jaguar Mark 9 parked in front of Lewells, a Morris Minor with split windscreen meaning it must an old 850, stands directly behind it. An A55 can be seen outside what is now the Examiner offices and a Mark 1 Ford is parked outside Crowther and Shaw. The car in the centre of the shot is a Humber Hawk.

Below: 'The Comancheros' starring John Wayne is on offer 'today' in 1962 at the Majestic on Viaduct Street. Regent Petrols are for sale at the garage opposite the cinema, at the left hand edge of the shot, and Pye Car Radios are advertised. Trolley bus cables form a network overhead and a Wolseley is parked outside the garage, facing the camera, with a Renault Caravelle parked across the road, facing away from the camera. 'Going to the pictures' was always a good night out. There was invariably a queue, a long queue for some films, and friends would bump into each other and enjoy a chat and a joke whilst waiting.

The famous 'back row' was always for courting couples as many readers may well remember! One local lady, now in her sixties, recalls getting through a bag of Rowntrees Mis-shapes, an ice cream and an ice lolly every time she went to the cinema and also recalls that she never got fat in those days! The young men would moon over Marilyn Monroe, Jennifer Jones and Gina Lollobrigida whilst the ladies swooned over Rock Hudson, Stewart Granger and of course, Huddersfield's own, James Mason. James was born in Marsh in 1909, the son of a wool merchant. He never forgot his Huddersfield roots and regularly visited his parents and his brother Rex. James Mason died in July, 1984 having spent his final years in Switzerland. His former home at Croft House Lane in Marsh has been demolished.

Right: Sombre and soot blackened, these buildings show us the appearance of a part of New Street in September 1956. Hammonds Boot and Shoe public house, centre of the shot, was a popular town centre pub and readers may remember enjoying Town Ales or possibly the landlord of the time, Stanley Thorpe, and his vociferous parrot who could both entertain and embarrass customers! When the street was redeveloped to create more shops the Boot and Shoe was moved into the basement and renamed the Shoehorn!

The ground floor businesses shown here are dramatically changed these days. The premises of Armitage & Sons Seed Growers are now occupied by the Ponden Mill Shop. Armitages now run Armitage Garden Centres at Birchencliffe and Shelley and are one of Huddersfields longest established businesses. They started out with a corn and seed warehouse in the Beast Market in 1842. Dixons now inhabit what used to be the bar of the Boot and Shoe but the hotel memory lingers on in the ornate stonework and inscription 'The Boot and Shoe Hotel' above the modern shop front. Flares nightclub comes next these days occupying what was the Boot and Shoes Wines and Spirits Store, the alleyway entrance to the right of the hotel. The Yorkshire Building Society are in the plot on the corner.

The Huddersfield ladies seen queuing lower left of this shot, waiting for the number six Crosland Moor bus, probably chose to sit downstairs. Readers may remember that the upper deck had a narrow aisle and long bench seats accommodating six passengers. The conductor passed tickets and change along the row and, sin of sins, smoking was allowed upstairs!

A view of Cloth Hall Street taken in March, 1954. The popular ABC Ritz cinema and restaurant can be seen clearly, centre shot, at the top of the street. The cinema was eventually demolished and Sainsbury's supermarket now stands on this site. At the top right hand corner of this photograph is GD Davies home decorating shop. Eagle-eyed readers can spot this store elsewhere in this book to give a clear perspective of this picture. Lower down Cloth Hall Street, right hand side looking at the photograph, a wall sign can be seen indicating the premises of Mr Morris Bray, photographer, whose work this photograph is. Parked

outside Mr Bray's premises is a Volkswagon Beetle with a split rear window, foreign cars would have been a rare sight in Huddersfield in those days. Guy Laycock's electrical shop, eventually taken over by Slaters, is next door to the photographers and below them the Halifax Building Society. The Halifax still occupies this site but their premises have been altered and enlarged beyond recognition from this shot. The White Hart public house, top left of the street on this shot, is still there but lower down on the left, how have Matthews Furs fared? Remember when it was acceptable, admirable even, to wear fur?

This nostalgic scene dates from July 1950. a young policeman looks out across the normally busy road to the corner of New Street and High Street, white gloves clasped tightly in his hand as an old man contemplates crossing the wide thoroughfare. To the right of the police officer, away from the position of the photographer, was one of the distinctive Huddersfield bus stops for passengers wishing to travel to Almondbury and Moldgreen. This was beneath the impressive, vertical *Prudential Assurance* sign which indicated the location of their Huddersfield office where an army of clerical staff would process policies and claims for the thousands of *Pru* customers residing in the town.

Far away in the distance the Burton's building can just be seen. The Leeds-based tailoring company had a tight grip on the market for ready-to-wear mens clothing at the time. Virtually every town and city of a respectable size boasted a similar Burtons store with similar styling and often a dance hall or snooker hall on the upper floor. Millions of pounds worth of property was acquired by the shrewd Burton family on the back of their success in the world of tailoring. Almost every self-respecting male can remember his first Burton's suit and the occasion, such as his first interview/wedding/ funeral etc. for which it was bought.

The trolley bus in this picture is quite interesting. It was one of a limited number seen on Britain's roads with a double rear axle which helped to spread the weight of its heavy load of passengers.

September 1953 and a view over St George's Square with the railway station in the background.

The famous George Hotel, birthplace of The Rugby League, can be seen at the left hand edge of this shot. A plaque in the bar commemorates the inaugural meeting of the Rugby League in 1895 and contains a fascinating display of memorabilia from the early days of the sport.

Working men who loved to play rugby were running into financial difficulties due to having to take time off work to train and play. As the Rugby Union were strictly amateur, the men broke away and formed the Rugby League which allowed for them to be paid for playing.

There has virtually always been a hotel on the site of the George. The present day hotel was built between 1845-

1850, the same period as the railway station, and replaced the much older George Inn which had been demolished to make way for the construction of John William Street and St Georges Square. The early 1900s saw the square as the venue for annual children's treat organised by the Huddersfield Sunday School Union.

Children were brought from all the churches and chapels in the town to parade and generally enjoy themselves with tea and games.

Britannia Buildings, across the square from the hotel, were constructed in 1856-59 and were built as warehouses and offices. For many years they were the home of the Huddersfield Building Society but are now owned by the Yorkshire Building Society.

Overhead trolley wires were still much in evidence when this delightful scene was captured, soon after the dawn of the 1960s. The people shown either relaxing, chatting or hurrying to the shops would be unaware that they were about to experience a decade of such tremendous change in everything from social values and attitudes to home entertainment, to transport and space travel.

The town centre of Huddersfield looks far too peaceful to ever be influenced by the dynamism that would characterise the 1960s. For everyone in Britain the pace of life was slower in these days, around four decades ago.

Some of the businesses shown in the picture may bring back memories of those times; Kendall's was the place to go if you wanted to keep dry with a selection of rainwear and umbrellas to suit the fashion-conscious of all ages. The licensed restaurant called The White House was popular at a time before many people took eating out for granted. Next to the sign promoting Mothers Pride bread was the underground gents' toilets. The whole area looks free from litter and graffiti - in fact the term graffiti was not even in common use at the time. Happy days indeed.

Below: A wide angle view of the buildings off High Street in 1957 before they were demolished to make way for the Civic Centre and the Law Courts. The old bus station on Upperhead Row can be seen just right of upper centre of the shot and is that a Halifax bus waiting to pull out? The new bus station incorporated Upperhead Row and the stands which used to be on Lord Street. The company in the bottom left hand corner of this shot is Broadbents and could be the TW Broadbents, Electrical Applicances, who eventually moved into the Imperial Arcade. Next door to Broadbents, Boultons Estate Agency can be seen, also moved but still trading in Huddersfield. From the roof of the Gas Showrooms, from where this photograph was taken, we can see a Rover driving in solitary splendour towards the bus stop.

The mill chimney, poking up against the skyline to the upper right of this shot , is no longer there but the shorter, squatter construction beside it is still in position. This latter is one of two vents which exist to channel smoke out from the railway. To the left of the vent is the outline of the interesting building which still is Spring Grove School.

Right: A beautifully clear shot of Huddersfield Railway Station in July 1964 - before the cleaning process had begun! The cleaning and restoration of this magnificent building, completed in 1995, actually cost more than the £2,000 it cost to build. Many readers will have happy memories of exciting times setting off from here on sunny August Saturdays at Huddersfield Holiday Week! However, rail fares soared in 1947 and a 3rd class monthly return to Blackpool would have set you back 19s 1d - 95p. Had you fancied a shopping expedition to Leeds, a monthly return would have cost you 4s 11d - 24p!

Bess, Dolly and Tommy were the last shire horses to be employed at Huddersfield railway station. All three were made redundant in 1952. The horses were all locally bred and had to weigh 15 cwt to qualify for railway work - magnificent animals but will you own up to remembering them?

The station, designed by JP Pritchett and completed in 1850, has been the subject of several famous quotes. Sir John Betjeman considered it one of the finest examples of railway architecture outside London and said it had the finest facade of any such building in the country, it has also been famously described as a stately home with trains in it! A major landmark in the town and a building of national importance. Huddersfield Railway Station is a Grade 1 listed building.

From 1873 until 1949 a statue of Sir Robert Peel stood outside the main entrance. His statue was removed as it was feared that Royal visitors arriving by rail would be offended to be greeted by Sir Robert's back.

Left: The junction of King Street, Cross Church Street and Queen Street, now a pedestrianised area. This photograph dates back to the 1960s.

Close scrutiny of Furnishall's windows will show a dralon covered armchair and a display of hearthrugs. The hearthrugs, in the window to the left of the door, have bold geometric patterns and are highly reminiscent of this period - remember all those old film sets of 'contemporary' interiors? Bright colours which didn't match or tone, button back armchairs and dining chairs with chromium legs! Hearthrugs were necessary, of course, in the days of coal fires. Fires could splutter and spit and send sparks onto carpets which needed protecting by rugs. Remember waking up on January morning with ice on the inside of the bedroom windows? Going downstairs, freezing cold, to light the fire? Sometimes the fire had been 'banked up' the previous night and could still be glowing - what relief! If not it meant tightly folding newspapers into thick 'sticks' and laying firewood on top to encourage the fire to life before adding too much coal. Firelighters could help too, a well known brand was 'Zippo' in their black box with the yellowish-orange flash of flame. How easy now to set a timer for the central heating or turn a switch on the gas fire. In the 1940s, making 'rag rugs' could involve the whole family. The backing could be stretched out between Mum, Dad and the children and, with a special knotting tool, strips of rag, often cut from old clothes, would be pushed through the backing fabric and 'knotted' to prevent loosening. These rag rugs were often artis-

tically designed with careful thought on the use of colour and were invariably attractive items. In later years rug kits came onto the market. These had stiff, white, large-meshed canvas backing sheets marked out with a design which could be embroidered in the thick wools provided. Candlewick became popular for rugs too, particularly in bathrooms and bedrooms. Furniture was always arranged around the fireplace because it was too cold to sit in any other part of the room!

Above: This temporary building for the Huddersfield branch of the Midland Bank was erected at the junction of Fox Street and Market Street whilst the old building in Cloth Hall Street was demolished and a new one built. In April, 1966 when this photograph was taken, the cherry trees to the right of the shot were in full bloom and really were 'pretty as a picture' - a pity that this shot wasn't in colour. Just off to the right of this photograph, the junction of Market Street with Westgate is known as Cherry Tree Corner because, in the last century, the Cherry Tree pub stood there. The planting of the cherry trees in this shot is likely to be the work of Mr Cowling who had a florists shop on the corner for many years. The cars parked in front of the bank are a Vauxhall Viva Mark One, right hand edge of the shot, behind it is a Hillman Minx followed by a Rover Coupe and the car at the back is thought to be a Riley. The rear end of a Wolseley 1500 can be seen in the bottom left hand corner of the frame. Riley and Hillman were both manufactured by the Roots Group which was subsequently taken over by Chrysler and then by General Motors.

Left: No, this photograph was not taken in the middle of the night with unbelievably effective lighting! It was taken in 1969 and this shot clearly illustrates the changes in traffic volumes over the last thirty years - look at the number of empty parking spaces in the bad old days!

The style and nature of the buildings in the foreground of this picture make them undeniably 1960s. This shot is taken from the roof of the Fire Station and shows the new Huddersfield Police Station on the right and the Law Courts on the left. The cars parked in the middle of this shot would now be very dangerously placed - in the middle of the ring road! The inner ring road hadn't been completed in June 1969, the date of this photograph, although it had been envisaged and pencilled in as a project and the eastern section completed. The official opening of the ring road was in November, 1973, marking its final completion.

The Co-op clock tower can be seen clearly against the skyline at the right hand edge of this shot and the spire of St Pauls is beside it. St Pauls is now a concert hall and forms part of Huddersfield University. Along to the left of St Pauls spire, the roof of the Town Hall is clearly defined against the lighter sky. The block of flats in the middle of this shot is Buxton House, between the Law Courts and the Police Station. The Courts and Police Station remain but the hoped for fountains and pools have never been put into place.

Above: The swinging sixties and the site of what was to be Huddersfields new market hall. The Town Hall/Concert Hall loftily looks down onto the muddy quagmire remaining after the demolition of the Police and Fire Stations. This photograph taken on May 16th, 1968, shows the town centre redevelopment plan well under way. In the distance, just behind the Town Hall, building work on Buxton House flats can be seen to be in progress. This was Phase Two of the redevelopment plan, the Civic Centre, Police Station and Law Courts comprising Phase One.

The last fire engines left the old Princess Street station in February 1961 and the old Police Station on Peel Street was replaced by a new building on Albion Street. In June, 1948, three of the police force's 'powerful' cars were fitted with radios and the public were being encouraged to report anything suspicious by using one of Huddersfield's 47 Police Boxes - later of Doctor Who fame!

In 1952 Huddersfield's police force comprised of 169 men and six women to police a population of 130,000, a ratio of one officer per 743 citizens.

The ration of police officers to citizens for the West Yorkshire Constabulary in 1996/7 was 2.4 per thousand. Not a great deal of change apart from the apparent increase in crime.

The new inner ring road is almost complete but one check remains - do the street lights work? As can be seen from this picture - they do! This shot is of the lighting tests on the almost finished road and is taken from the Fire Station looking towards Trinity Street. One of the Technical College buildings can be seen behind the Morris Minor coming towards the camera. Vital statistics of the new road include the cost of £3,570,000, three-quarters of which came from the Department of the Environment. Approximately 169 traffic signs and 60 bollards were needed and 214,000 cubic yards of bulk excavation was involved which included 100,000 cubic yards from the disused railway cutting at Fartown.

Three sections of under-surface heating were installed - at the steep approach gradient to the Chapel Hill junction, the slip road from New North Road to the ring road and the approach and exit ramps of the underpass. The principal contractors were Dowsett Engineering Construction of Harrogate. An objective in planning the new road was to keep traffic and pedestrians safely away from each other and various crossing points, controlled by lights were built into the planning along with a footbridge. Nowadays three pedestrian subways, giving access to the Technical College, to and from the Bus Station and crossing Southgate, ensure the safety of pedestrians when crossing the ring road.

Above: An interesting picture here. A view of what was to become the town's first underpass - Unna Way - framed by the old stone of the railway arch. The shot is taken looking towards Southgate. Unna Way is named after Huddersfield's twin town in Germany and the underpass carries the east bound carriageway of the road under Bradford Road and the Northgate junction.

The people of Huddersfield may have been keen to do a lap of the new inner ring road in 1973, the year it was finally completed. If they'd wanted to buy a car to test out the new tarmac a 1973 Vauxhall Victor, one owner, 10,000 miles on the clock, would have set them back to the tune of £1,295. An immaculate fastback Sunbeam Rapier with overdrive dating from 1971 would have carried a £995 price tag and an automatic Hillman Avenger 1500 from the same year could be yours for £845. But, if it had to be brand new, a Robin Reliant Super Saloon, averaging 60 miles per gallon at 40 miles per hour would have cost £848.46! You could have had a top of the range Motorola 124 LM radio fitted for £12.50 and driven off along the new road to meet friends taking six bottles of Websters Green Label for 36p and a four pack of Babycham for 33p. As Grandad used to say - you could have a good night out and come home with change from a tanner!

Right: Besancon Bridge, but not in Besancon it's in Huddersfield! The bridge gives access over the ring road to the town centre. This photograph shows the bridge nearing completion during the excavations for the building of the new inner ring road. Company 'rationalisation' and reductions in staff are a modern phenomenon but this lonely workman looks to have his work cut out!

The bridge is named after Huddersfield's twin town in France and carries Fitzwilliam Street over the inner ring road to a junction with John William Street and Viaduct Street. Fitzwilliam Street Church can be seen at the right hand edge of this shot to give perspective to the angle of the view.

The idea of an inner ring road was first raised in 1954. The complexities of settling on the best route took around seven years and the eastern half of the road was finally completed in 1963. Ten years later the planners' dreams came to fruition with the final, western, stage reaching completion. The road was opened on November 2nd, 1973 and a commemorative plaque can be seen on a wall near to the Technical College and beside the new road. Earlier in the same year, 1973, the local press had reported disappointment that the completion of the M62 had only reduced traffic into Huddersfield by around one fifth. At the time the road was opened, Alderman Eric Whittaker, chairman of the Highways Committee, admitted that the road wouldn't solve all the town's problems but it was generally felt that the road was a big step forward in the battle against traffic congestion.

Sporting life

Above: The cup-winning Huddersfield Rugby League Team with the committee in May 1953. It is of course Fartown! No-one has ever called the Huddersfield side by their correct title but always by their nickname of Fartown which derives from where they played until around 1991.

The team seen here have won the Rugby League Challenge Cup, (left) and the Yorkshire Cup, (right).

The players are, from the back row, (standing):-
J Brown, W Griffin, J Bowden, J Large, J Cooper, E Slevin, DD Valentine, (middle row) R Cracknell, P Henderson, JC Hunter, GR Pepperell, L Cooper, P Devery, R Rylance (Capt), (front row) W Banks, P Ramsden

As is well known, Huddersfield played a crucial role in the formation of the Rugby League or Norther Union as it was known until the early 1920s. Working men needed the 'broken time payments' for time taken off work to train or travel to games. The true amateurs of the Rugby Union wouldn't accept any kind of payment and the Union faced with defiant Huddersfield players, threatened and subsequently expelled Huddersfield. The Huddersfield club however already had several other clubs interested in joining them in the formation of the Northern Union and the momentous meeting took place in the George Hotel in St George Square, Huddersfield in 1895. The hotel bar has a commemorative plaque and an interesting collection of memorabilia.

Right: The gentlemen champions of Slaithwaite Bowling Club with their trophies in September 1959. The popular vehicles of the time, parked in the background of the shot, are a Lambretta scooter, a Renault Caravelle, an Austin A30, Austin Cambridge and a Reliant Robin.

A little known fact about Slaithwaite is that it once attracted visitors from all over Lancashire and Yorkshire and was a very busy town between 1825 and 1925. Early records of Slaithwaite show that the manor was owned by Kirklees Priory and that one Henry Tyas paid a mark, around 66p, for the use of the mill circa 1211.

Dr Beeching and his dramatic cuts to the railways were very unpopular with Slaithwaite 'Anorak' Mr Donald Sykes who, as a schoolboy, enjoyed sitting on the station wall trainspotting as he went home from school at dinner-time. The station closed and the steam trains stopped in the early 1960s.

Slaithwaite Methodist Church Amateur Operatic Society has featured large in Slaithwaite life for many years and will be celebrating their 50th anniversary in 1999 with a special October performance. Mr Sykes recalls the concert arranged in celebration of the Queen's Silver Jubilee when, playing to a packed Civic Hall, the man standing next to him, who was a soloist, whispered 'am I on next'? 'Yes,' replied Mr Sykes. The soloist carefully moved into position during the final bars of the previous item and began to give a full-voiced rendition only to find the accompanist on the piano was playing a totally different tune! He was quietly told, 'not now Frank'!

Above: There are not too many children watching this event - the 'Mum's Race' at the ICI Children's Gala in June 1957. You weren't too happy about your Mum entering the race, what if she did something silly, like tripping up, and embarrassed you in front of all your friends! Sprinting and competing wasn't the sort of thing you expected your Mum to do. Although one brave young boy, right of the shot, is running alongside apparently to encourage his Mum. There was always that tiny spark of hope though, what if your Mum won? Or even if she made a good effort - how proud you would have been! These young women certainly seem to be enjoying the fun of the race. They've thrown off their shoes, stopped worrying about laddering their stockings, pulled up their skirts and gone for the line. Ladies, do you remember the restrictive nature of feminine underwear in the 1950s?

was first opened in 1893 and had a fleet of 30 rowing boats and a pleasure steamer named 'Nil Desperandum'! In 1947 Hope Bank was taken over by Fred Thompson of Cleveley who installed speed boats, a helter skelter and a small zoo. A record crowd of 50,000 attended Hope Bank on Whit Monday in 1948 which fell on May 18th. It seems strange nowadays to think about 'moveable feasts' when we are used to the holiday, now called Spring Bank Holiday, always being the last Monday in May. Tasha the bear from Hope Bank Zoo escaped in January 1951 and although the RSPCA made many attempts to recapture her it proved impossible and she had to be shot as darkness approached. Hope Bank closed in 1955 having lost its popularity and the lake was drained and the site used for the building of new premises for Brook Motors.

Top: The 'Holidays at Home' programme of entertainments covered a wide range of activities for those Huddersfield folk who decided to stay put for the Holiday Week. This photograph shows a bowling tournament in progress in Greenhead Park in August 1953. Huddersfield 'Holidays at Home' began in 1941 to entertain those who couldn't get away because of the war. The idea really took off and the events ranged from a simple game of giant draughts in the park to talent contests and shows.

Hope Bank at Honley would have been a popular destination for a day out for many Huddersfield families. It

Above left: It is the ICI Children's Gala in June 1962 and the boys are racing away in competition for the title of 'Winner of the Sack Race'! It looks as if one contestant arrived a little late and other boys are saying 'Please Sir, let me have a go', foreground of the shot, slightly right of centre and the boys clustering round a suited man, perhaps he was the 'starter'. To the left of this frame a group of three girls, two of them wearing party style hats, are huddled with arms around each other no doubt giggling at the boys and their particular favourite! Some things never change!

Shopping spree

'Boots Corner' and a fascinating photograph here, so much to see and so many memories just waiting to be aroused. More correctly, this shot shows the Devonshire Buildings at the junction of King Street and Victoria Lane in the early 1950s. The clothes worn by the people in the picture seem formal by today's standards - not a pair of denims in sight and it's flat caps rather than baseball caps in this decade. The next shop up, to the right of this shot, is Montague Burtons 'The Tailor of Taste'. Burton's appears very modern when compared with the soot blackened Boots building and its crowded window displays. The window below the word 'prescriptions' contains, in the bottom left hand corner, what could be soap bags or, on the other hand, they could be nightdress cases. Did you ever embroider one as a gift for someone? Do you remember folding your nightgown neatly and placing it in the soft, fabric case and laying it on the pillow? Satin cases in jewel colours were always prized and, total luxury, a case in quilted satin! Eiderdowns covered our beds, not duvets.

No-one walking down this street at the time this photograph was taken would have the vaguest idea what a duvet was! The eiderdowns were square, the size of the top of the bed and were often in quilted satin, deep red was a popular colour with an embroidered motif in the centre. There was nothing like snuggling down beneath the weight of woollen blankets between clean, thick cotton sheets which smelt of fresh air and ironing. On the other hand, the sheets and blankets could have smelt like camphor if they'd been stored in a chest with mothballs for protection! Fennings Fevercure could have been bought here, a light brown powder in a folded white paper with the company logo on the front. You either loved the taste or hated it. Maybe your Mum gave you a teaspoonful of liquid paraffin each week to make sure you .... do you remember? Or perhaps you were given sulphur and treacle on a spoon to rid you of teenage spots or ensure you never got them! In the window to the left of the door is a display of vacuum flasks. Huddersfield folk may recall using them on picnics at Hope Bank, Honley or Sunny Vale - didn't the sun always shine?

Some of the big-guns in national retailing can be seen in this photograph of New Street. Among these popular shops was F.W. Woolworth & Co - or Woollies as most of us knew it - seen here with extended sun shades to protect the goods in the window and keep the temperature down to tolerable levels inside the store. Stylo was an up-to-date shoe retailer on New Street and, again, the name could be seen on most decent high streets throughout the land. If the heat got too much then a short walk down the passage next to Stylo would lead you to 'The Albert' where refreshing Town Ales would revive you.

If beer was considered inappropriate then coffee or tea could be enjoyed at the cafe above Collinsons further along the street. The picture was taken in 1953, a time when New Street could become very congested as through traffic mingled with vehicles making deliveries to busy shops. This was an era before the introduction of parking meters, 'yellow lines' and the first Traffic Warden had yet to be spotted on Huddersfield's streets. As the number of vehicles grew it was inevitable that multi-storey car parks and strict rules and regulations governing parking would be introduced in this and similar towns throughout Britain.

Huddersfield's High Street Buildings stand proudly, rather like the prow of a ship, in the forefront of this photograph taken in December 1969. High Street leads upwards to the right of this shot and Buxton Road, now New Street, leads off to the left. The number 2 bus to Golcar via Leymoor is halted at the pedestrian crossing on High Street. This model is an AEC whilst the bus coming along Buxton Road, outside C & A, is a Daimler. A Ford car can be seen driving up High Street which, of course, cannot happen these days, the one-way system only allows driving down High Street. In the background, behind C & A, Buxton House flats poke up against the sky and part of the Civic Centre can be seen at the right hand edge of the shot. Red Circle Libraries, left of centre in this picture, have disappeared to be replaced by a shop selling pictures and picture frames. Buxton Road is, as previously mentioned, now New Street and a pedestrianised shopping precinct. The Huddersfield Co-op is situated just off to the left of this shot. These are the days when it was acceptable to advertise cigarettes and smoking was a widespread habit. The tobacconists shop on the corner of Buxton Road and High Street boldly advertises Capstan cigarettes but they are 'Medium' and not 'Full Strength'!

Above: This photograph will evoke many a memory among Huddersfield people. It shows the businesses and buildings along what was Buxton Road, now New Street, as they were in September 1950. This section of the road is that from the High Street Buildings, the corner just visible at the right hand edge of the shot, down to the Curzon Cinema and the entire plot is now occupied by C & A. The Curzon was once known as the Picturedrome and one Huddersfield man, Mr Ben Whittaker, recalls being thrown out on many occasions for being rowdy and throwing toffee papers around! This bad lad remembers going to see the original King Kong at the Picturedrome. A western appears to be showing at the Curzon in September 1950, 'A Ticket to Tomahawk'. Remember buying your footwear from Cable Shoes, centre of this shot? Readers may also remember McKitrick Bros Mill Furnishers and Tool Dealers believed to have been situated beyond the Curzon, off to the left of this shot. Mr Trevor Brennan, proprietor of Wellington Mills Joinery and a Huddersfield man, recalls their distinctive and very old shop frontage. Central steps were flanked by square bay windows with small square panes of glass. The frontage was painted in green on either side. Metal railings stood outside. Next door to McKitrick Bros in 1949 was a chemist selling cough mixture for 1s 5d. Can you work that one out in 'new' money?

Right: A familiar sight for Huddersfield people here. Winn's Poultry shops on a corner site in Victoria Street on the outside of the old Huddersfield Market Hall as it was in May, 1961. Remember when roast chicken was an expensive treat? The poster in the large window, left of shot, advertises Winn's Rotiss-o-mat and the fact that chicken is the meal you can afford indicative of the period when chicken was becoming an everyday and affordable meat. Winn's was also famous for selling quality and unusual fish, for example shark, and eventually moved from this site to premises in the new market hall. They have only recently closed down. Bottom right of this shot is the beginning of The Shambles which ran up towards the left of this photograph but cannot be seen in this shot.

In the days before refrigeration this was a popular spot for a Saturday evening stroll and shopping. The tradesmen had to sell off all their goods, they wouldn't keep until Monday, and many bargains, flowers, greengrocery as well as meat, could be had!

Remember wearing headscarves ladies? A couple of the Huddersfield housewives in this shot are emulating the Royals by wearing them. Headsquares, as they were often known locally, were often twisted into turbans in the 1940s and early 50s and, if you'd run out of better ideas, were popular gifts for birthdays and Christmas.

A well known sight to Huddersfield shoppers here. Wallaces Ltd, King Street. Selling groceries, confectionery, general provisions and offering Quality and Service. Nescafe was on special offer at 2s 9d per tin, four pounds of sugar could be had for the special price of 2s 5d and Apple and Raspberry jam was a real bargain at 1s 1d.

This photograph was taken in the late fifties when there were 12 pennies to the shilling, 240 pennies or 20 shillings to the pound - so how much are the products mentioned in 'new money'?

In case those calculations made your head spin, the Nescafe would equate to around 13p, the sugar 12.5p and the jam 5p. The shop windows are literally

crammed with items for sale as were the windows of most shops in those days. Modern window displays seem almost stark by comparison but we are no longer recovering from the deprivations of a war, a possible explanation for the crowded style of window display in the fifties. It certainly made window shopping worthwhile!

The Kingsway Café, above Wallaces, offered luncheons, teas and suppers and was a popular meeting place. On each side of Wallaces are Marks and Spencers and H & J Wilson's clothing store. The Vauxhall Cresta parked at the kerb, lower right edge of this shot, indicates that traffic was still permitted on King Street and no-one had dreamt that it would ever become a traffic free zone.

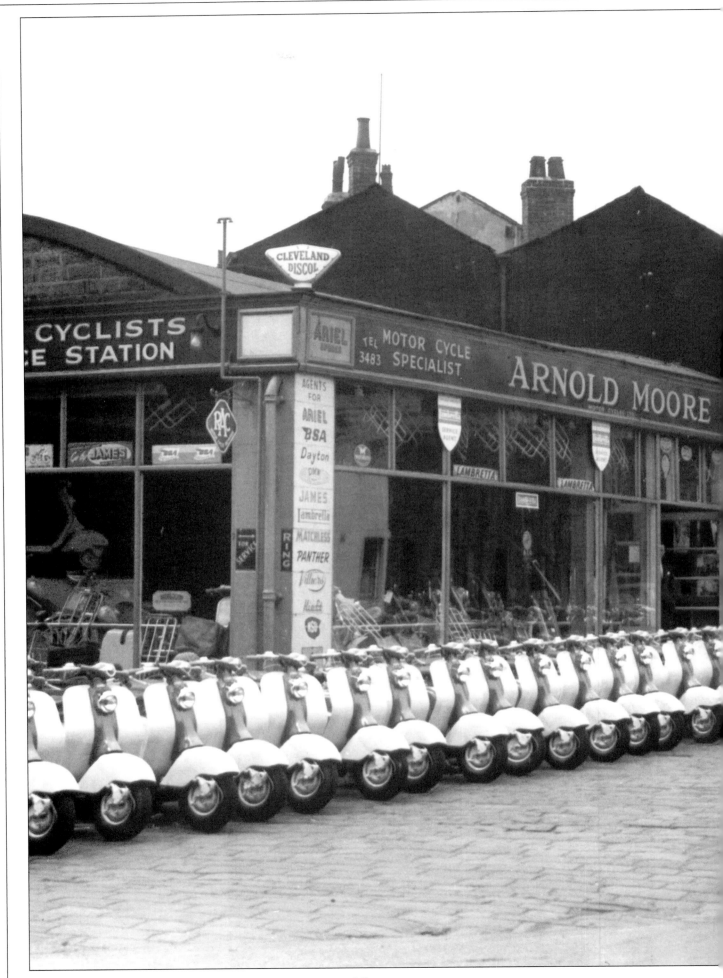

On the move

Left: Arnold Moore's Oxford Street garage in May 1957 and no prizes for guessing what he had for sale! Lambrettas were extremely popular at this time - and to this day hold an attraction for scooter enthusiasts who still get together and hold rallies. This was the time of the Suez crisis and petrol rationing which could explain the initial popularity of the scooter. Lambrettas were designed and manufactured in one factory in Italy owned by a Mr Innocenti but they became so popular and demand so great that the company opened factories in Spain and India to try and meet orders. Ultimately India bought out the rights to Lambretta and now they are only manufactured in that country.

During the fifties Italian styling became fashionable and gentlemen may remember wearing 'Italian' style suits and shoes. How many readers can remember buying Cleveland Discol at Moores? They were agents for Ariel, BSA, Dayton, Janes, Matchless, Panther and other motor bikes as well as Lambretta scooters.

The ladies always like scooters because it wasn't necessary to sit astride them so they accomodated the skirts of the time, and many of them had small white 'shopping' baskets attached. Originally they were a trendy mode of transport amongst the younger set who would feel 'cool' to be seen driving one!

Below: The old Bus Station at Upperhead Row in almost the same spot as the new Bus Station but totally different. A very functional construction which appears grim and very basic in this shot when compared with the attractive trappings of the modern day version.

A corner of the Town Hall can be seen on the upper right hand edge of the shot and is that the George Hotel on the horizon to the left of the cooling towers? The top of the spire of the old Market cane be seen outlined against the sky to the right of the cooling towers and a large crane. Readers will find 20/20 vision essential though! The old market building is much missed by Huddersfield people. The placards at the back of the bus station are advertising Kit-Kat and 'My Goodness My Guiness' - the last slogan will stir a few memories. The Huddersfield public transport system set up shop with one steam engine and one passenger car on January 11th 1883 - the original tram service. Permission to operate a motor bus service in Huddersfield was first obtained from the Board of Trade in 1913. However the intervention of the First World War meant that the first bus to actually run was on December 18th 1920. The route was Paddock Head to Golcar and the bus was a single decker made by Karrier Motors Ltd, a local firm. Trams, trolley buses and motor buses ran concurrently for several years. Huddersfield was the first municipal authority in Britain to run and operate a public transport system.

Above: Viaduct Street in March, 1953 and Newton's Filling Station fills the foreground. On this site nowadays stands the Tesco Filling Station occupying virtually the same spot. To the right of this shot was the junction of Viaduct and John William Streets. Readers may remember the once familiar curving frontage of Ripon Bros the agents for Rolls Royce which used to stand on that corner.

For many years Newton's was the only filling station which was open for 24 hours. The demand for an 'all hours' service just wasn't there in the early 1950s. The pump attendant therefore had another job - valeting cars at the back of the premises. Mr Morris Bray, perhaps Huddersfield's best known photographer who took this shot, recalls that there was a bell for late night customers. The actual bell was so far away that the customer couldn't hear it ring and would only know it had worked when the boiler-suited and wellington booted attendant appeared in the distance heading slowly towards you across the vastness of the showroom. The attendant would have to let himself out of the showroom, unlock the kiosk, switch on the pumps and only then could he serve you with petrol. Self-service was unheard of in those days and Mr Bray, whilst not wanting to hurt the modern day motorist, also recalls that in the late 1940s he regularly bought four gallons and had change from a ten bob (50p) note!

Mr Newton was a well known local businessman who, before the war, used to import large American cars. In the 1950s these cars were all stored in a large four storey building which stood across the road from the filling station as seen in this shot. Mr Ben Whittaker , a Huddersfield man, recalls that he and a friend were once allowed to go into the building and drool over these vast, impractical but much admired vehicles. Mr Whittaker lost his heart to a silver blue Plymouth which was waiting to be checked over before delivery to a customer. He later came across this same car featured in a magazine article and was shocked to see the object of his desire described as the kind of car an American plumber's mate would buy for his wife!

Right: The Brockholes Motor Company on Westgate as it was in 1962. A sixties style, modern construction amongst the older victorian buildings on the street. Brockholes is now known as Arriva and is situated near to the McAlpine Stadium. Soon after the war, this site was occupied by a furniture shop which was eventually destroyed by fire. It is believed that later came Malglades who sold garden products and equipment. The store now on this site sells denim jeans and fashionable, trendy clothing.

A Ford Popular, clearly labelled by the registration plate, pokes out from the doorway of Brockholes showroom. These basic, affordable cars were ultimately replaced by the Ford Anglia an example of which can be seen to the left of the Popular. In the right hand showroom window is a Ford Consul Estate which was a more upmarket model in the Ford range. A Road Fund licence would have set you back around £10 in those days.

Above: Concrete Utilities Ltd of Ware in Hertfordshire, the owners of the lorry in the foreground, probably didn't know that weather like this existed. But this is 'up t'north' in 1953 and 'by 'eck t'weather wer bad'!

It's to be hoped there were no horses in the vehicle behind the wagon. The winter a decade later in 1963 is said to have been equally bad but many will recall the winter of 1947-8 as being the worst of all. Mr Morris Bray the Huddersfield photographer recalls receiving telephone calls from national newspapers advising him of cars and wagons being stuck in snow at Standedge or Holme Moss and being asked to take photographs of the arctic conditions. The last part of his trek had to be on foot of course, and he recalls the weight of his camera and glass negatives in those days. It was very hard going. On one occasion he believed he had damaged his eyes when his vision would be perfect from one angle and blurred from another. Only when he finally got back to his car did he discover that it was icicles hanging from his eyelashes that were responsible for the problem!

> *The snowfall was particularly bad in January 1952 and volunteers were called in with shovels to keep the roads open*

because of the likeness to Edwardian dress worn by the boys), and Mr Whittaker can remember that his soles would melt from the heat from the exhaust of his motor bike!

These days drivers wouldn't be so well wrapped up because the heaters in their cars are so efficient. On the other hand it wouldn't matter because they wouldn't have to tramp through the snow to find a telephone, they would probably have a mobile. In any case we just don't get snow like this any more - or is that tempting fate?

Above: Abandoned vehicles on the A62 at Standedge in March 1953. The appropriate adjective is probably not a word but brrrrr! Imagine walking or rather plodding your way through this to the nearest telephone. As cars in those days didn't have heaters the drivers were no doubt well wrapped up. Hopefully they were wearing their heavy overcoats from the '50/- Tailors', as Burtons was known. These huge coats had extremely wide shoulders supported by lots of padding. They had buckled belts and were ankle length. Mr Ben Whittaker, a Huddersfield man, can recall having one in a green check fabric although they came in all kinds of colours. Wearing them in a snowstorm however, could have caused problems. When these coats were wet they were so heavy that the wearer couldn't move! Crepe soled shoes were also popular around this time of the 'Teddy Boy', ('Teddy'

Top: It's January 1952 and this huge snowplough is doing its best to keep the way to Holme Moss television station open. The snowfall was particularly bad in January of this year at Holme Moss and workmen and volunteers also had to do their bit with shovels to try and keep the road open. This was neither the first nor the last time they had or would be cut off by snow. The people who worked at Holme Moss kept a stock of food supplies and blankets to see them through any periods when they might be cut off from the rest of the world. The BBC supplied a mini-bus service for the workers at Holme Moss. Mr H Armitage was one of the drivers on that service and he was well used to battling his way through all but the most severe of weather conditions. The majority of Holme Moss staff would rely on the mini-bus for supplies, mail and getting to and from the station. A scare about the safety of television sets was reported in The Huddersfield Daily Examiner and widely across the country four months after this photograph was taken. A four year old child had been killed after coming into contact with the metal loudspeaker grille of the family's television set.

Above: The unmistakable sight of New Hey Road, one of the most historic of Huddersfield's roads, dating from the 1830s when it was created as part of the Turnpike Road Acts. The road formed an important connection between Huddersfield, Oldham and Rochdale from that time on. The photograph was taken in July 1938, the car in the foreground being typically curvaceous as we would expect of the period. Close inspection of the original print with a powerful magnifying glass revealed that the registration number of the vehicle was BCX 23. Enquires suggest that the car was registered new in March 1938, making it just a few months old when the picture was taken. The other car looks more typical of the 1920s, with its wire wheels and 'boxy' construction. Even more interesting than the vehicles shown are the pristine semi-detached houses with their immaculate stonework and pleasant Yorkshire stone garden walls. Again, it is known that these houses were only recently built (by the respected local builder, Wadsworths) and the first occupiers only just moved in. It is possible, indeed likely, that the picture was taken to mark the completion of the house-building project by someone connected with Wadsworth's. Local advertising material from the day informs us that the houses had been up for sale for the extremely reasonable price of £500 each - plus another £20 if a garage was required. They would cost well over 100 times that amount in modern times!

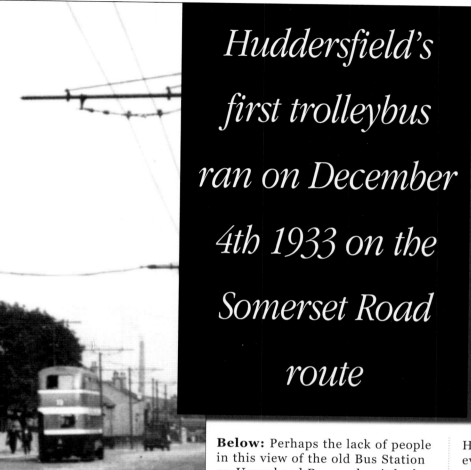

Huddersfield's first trolleybus ran on December 4th 1933 on the Somerset Road route

fare badly. Plenty of buses but apparently no passengers here, it's not like that these days, especially at peak hours. Trolley bus cables make a network overhead.

Huddersfield's first trolley bus ran on December 4th 1933 on the Somerset Road route. When the decision was made to end the trolley bus service and news of the final run became known, so many people turned out to ride on this popular form of transport for the very last time that the corporation had to provide an additional four trolley buses - and they were all full.

The final and fifth bus was reserved for the Mayor and civic dignitaries who also wanted to be included on the last trolley bus.

The route taken was Westgate to Waterloo and the whole of the route was packed with crowds watching the end of 37 years of trolley buses in Huddersfield. The highest point ever reached by a trolley bus anywhere in this country was Outlane.

The new Bus Station was officially opened on March 26th 1974 and operations began from there in December of that year.

Below: Perhaps the lack of people in this view of the old Bus Station on Upperhead Row makes it look so grim and forbidding. Or perhaps it is the comparison with the hustle and bustle and the colourful accoutrements of the new Bus Station which make the old one

Schooldays

Above: 'I wouldn't mind winning that'! The prizes on display at the ICI Children's Gala in June 1957. First prize for the 9 and 10 year old girls 80 yards flat handicap was a bagatelle game. In case you've forgotten, you pulled a button attached to a rod and a spring which sent a ball spinning wildly around pins in order to score points. A good prize in 1957 - probably the nearest thing to a Game Boy! Other prizes include a Sooty Stencil Set, a Pet Set, a gingerbread baking kit, an embroidery set and a toy weaving loom. Popular prizes judging by the rapt attention they are receiving but these are prizes for girls - not politically correct in these days of equality and unisex interests and hobbies. Children's Galas were annual events organised by many local companies. Ice Cream vans, sack races and roundabouts, laughing at Mum as she stumbled in the Mum's race or incredible amounts of pride if your Mum won! In those days you didn't think of Mums having any kind of athletic ability. They were sedentary creatures who made the sandwiches before the day out and then sat on a grassy bank whilst Dad organised the games and the rough and tumble. After making sure everyone was up and ready, preparing the picnic, making breakfast and then clearing it away, Mum was probably exhausted long before the outing began.

Right: The tea tent at the ICI Children's Gala in June 1956. Who can you spot on this

photograph? Remember these bright faced youngsters will be in their early fifties now! Cake, jelly and a chocolate wafer biscuit seems to be the tea-time treat along with a hot cup of tea on what appears to have been a wet day judging by the spattered raincoats being worn.

The weather doesn't appear to have dampened any spirits though. If Huddersfield folk allowed summer rain to spoil their fun they'd never have any!

These children would all have been born after the war, their Mums would have lived and possibly worked through it and their Dads may have seen action in one of the armed services. After the war government surplus clothing may have been the last thing Huddersfield Dads wanted to wear but, by 1951, there were bargains to be had in Milletts Store in Huddersfield. Slightly store soiled khaki shorts for 12s 6d, (62.5 new pence), or a military style raincoat at prices from 83s 5d to 119s 2d, (£4.18 to £5.96).

These youngsters would have been too young for National Service. Some readers may remember waiting for the brown envelope to drop through the letter box, going to Bradford for the medical. If the medical was passed there was more waiting to find out your fate - where would you be sent and to do what? National Service ended at around the time this photograph was taken, the late fifties.

Well wrapped up against the cold January weather, these children with their identity 'ribbons' and expressions of anticipation are arriving at the ABC Cinema for the ICI January 1962 Children's treat. These are the days before jeans and joggers took over the fashion scene and knee socks and boots were considered sufficient protection against what appears to be a cold and misty day. It is unlikely nowadays that a young boy would go out in short pants in January or a young girl in a skirt. The little girl standing second from right of this shot is wearing a hat that many readers may remember wearing or knitting. Often made with fluffy angora wool, and an Alice Band was threaded through a seam around the front which held the hat close to the head for warmth. A good idea we may have forgotten? The shop sign of GD Davies can be seen through the glass doors of the cinema and readers may remember buying the odd tin of paint or roll of wallpaper there. A Huddersfield man, Ray Hoyle, can remember being an ABC Minor and can recall, (almost), the words of the Saturday morning song.

Children being given attractively wrapped Christmas presents at the ICI Children's Treat at the Ritz cinema in Huddersfield, January 1957. Were you there? The little boy in the foreground, who will be in his forties now, couldn't wait to open his parcel. The photograph shows that he received a box of Bellamy's sweets. The school cap worn by the boy at the right hand edge of the shot will remind gentlemen readers of the days when it was compulsory! These lads and lasses possibly became big fans of the Beatles and Cliff Richard who both appeared in person at the Ritz as did Norman Wisdom. Did these young girls ever become part of the screaming, almost hysterical hordes of teenage girls who met the Beatles every appearance. Readers may remember that phenomenon never to be seen since.

Children from poorer families were sometimes given complimentary tickets to the Ritz and some readers may admit to being old enough to remember the song sheets and the bouncing ball depicting the words of the song! The organ was a Wurlitzer and the weekend organist at the Ritz at one period was Mr Leslie Bishop and 'By the Light of the Silvery Moon' was a favourite song whilst you watched a programme of the main feature, a 'B' movie, the Pathe news and a cartoon.

Above: This lively bunch look to be enjoying themselves enormously at the David Brown Gear Works Children's party in January, 1954. The paper cups probably contain pop or orange squash and carry the logo 'David Browns'. The rapidly emptying plates have been full of 'sticky bread', sandwiches and fancy cakes and the children are at various stages of tucking into jelly and ice cream in the small dishes. What would they do next? Disco dancing with strobe lights and a disc jockey? Unlikely. A game of 'London Bridge is Falling Down' perhaps or entertainment put on by a magician or a clown? In those days we enjoyed colouring with crayola crayons in a black box which had holes in it so that the crayons would stand up whilst in use. We had dolls with home made dolls clothes and houses. We made furniture for the dolls houses from match boxes glued together, covered in paper or fabric, (not sticky back plastic), to make armchairs and settees. If our creation were to be a

chest of drawers we would use gold metal paper fasteners to make knobs. We had Post Office sets and loved the special ones with ink pads and rubber stamps. Dads made or bought wooden forts with drawbridges and castellated towers. Corkwork was a hobby which produced a length of rope-like coloured fine wool. An empty bobbin, of the type which had held sewing thread, was needed and four tiny tacks knocked into the top. Fine wool was wrapped around the tacks and pulled through the bole in the bottom of the bobbin. The wool 'ropes' could be coiled and stitched into mats. We had Lotto, Snakes and Ladders and Ludo and, if we were really good, we could stay up and listen to 'Journey into Space' on the radio.

Top: A very special guest at this Christmas party - Santa Claus himself is seated in the middle of this happy photograph surrounded by smiling children. The presents have clearly been given out and the little boy with the wide grin in the foreground has received a 'Lucky Sport Car'. Other children have been given a Rustler Ace Rifle, a construction set and there are one or two baby dolls being cuddled. The Christmas tree in the background of the shot is decorated with tinsel and baubles as Christmas trees are today. In the fifties, ten years before this photograph was taken, many Huddersfield families didn't have electric fairy lights. Clip-on holders held wax candles, they looked beautiful when lit but the fire hazard!
Christmas morning would see the children out and about riding new Raleigh bikes and wearing hand knitted bobble caps and mittens and possibly feeling sick from eating chocolate at dawn when they'd woken up to see if 'he had been'! This photograph shows the Christmas party arranged for the children of the employees of J Goulder and Sons of Kirkheaton in December 1967.

Below right: What a spread has been put on by the Mums and Grans of the Outlane Bowling Club for the children's Christmas party of December 1953. A chocolate cake decorated with smarties and Santa, jam tarts, cups of tea and fruit and jelly in flower-shaped greaseproof paper dishes with coloured edges. Remember them?

Christmas is and always has been an exciting time for children. Christmas dinner is still usually turkey and brussel sprouts, pudding and mince pies. Sitting drowsily silent whilst everyone gathered round to listen to or watch the Queen and entertaining Grandma and Granddad is still the norm in many Huddersfield households. What Father Christmas brings down the chimney to well behaved children however has changed considerably since the 1950s. A 'selection box' would appear in many a stocking. These were not the brightly wrapped Cadbury's or Rowntrees chocolate bars which we see today. They were often pieces of chocolate, unwrapped or in plain coloured foil paper, and moulded into shapes for example a smoker's set would have included a pipe, matches and cigarettes all made of chocolate! Sweet cigarettes were common! Not any more - for obvious reasons. Boys would look for the Eagle Annual and most children enjoyed the Beano or Dandy comic book annuals. Licourice sets were also often brought by Santa, 'shoelaces' or strips of licourice coiled with a brightly coloured sugary sweet in the middle. Some licourice sticks had tops covered in 'hundreds and thousands' which were also sprinkled on the traditional tea-time trifle. As now, children were taken to Santa's grotto in a large store and were given a present before they hung up their stockings - which were rarely stockings but more usually white pillowcases.

Below: Primrose Hill Methodist Church can be seen in the background of this shot taken on the corner of Stile Common Road and Malvern Road. Standing off to the left of this shot would give a view over the woods of Ashenhurst and Lowerhouses. The crowd are waiting to see the procession because it is Primrose Hill Gala Day in July 1953. Everyone must have expected the procession to be good judging by those who have clambered onto roofs and walls, centre left of this shot, to watch it pass by.

What is intriguing though is what has happened just off the shot to the right. Has someone fallen? The two policemen appear to be going to help and a man in the middle of the road is bending over some thing or someone. Were you there?

At around the same time as this shot was taken, the ABC Ritz in Huddersfield was showing 'Tom Browns Schooldays' starring Robert Newton with 'Bandit Queen' to complete the double bill and, of course, the organ! A couple of months before this photograph was taken the newspapers had been advertising 'Rommel's own Story' as a means of attracting readers. Even eight years after the end of the war, it was still making the headlines. Most important of all, Huddersfield Town bounced back into Division 1 after having suffered relegation for the first time in 1952.

It's an old Austin Atlantic Convertible, on the left hand edge of the shot, it's the Netherton bus, top centre shot, and it's Meltham Co-op Gala and Field Day in June 1953. The group of lively lads in the foreground appear to be well protected, or is that controlled, by the men alongside the loosely formed column.

A plaque found in a Marsden garage in March, 1966 supplies evidence that the Meltham Co-op predated that of the Rochdale Pioneers. Meltham Co-op closed in 1969 but had been in existence since 1827. It began in a house in Shady Row, part of the Jonas Brook Mills complex, and moved two years later to to a shop in Meltham Mills Road. One of the early members took the idea to Rochdale having walked there to get a job. The plaque, which was once displayed in Meltham Mills Co-op,

read:- Meltham Mills Provident Co-operative Trading Society Limited Established 1827. (Believed to be the first Co-operative Society to pay Dividend on Purchases). Amalgamated in 1927 with Meltham Industrial Co-operative Society Limited forming Meltham and Meltham Mills Co-operative Society Limited.

Readers may remember the Meltham Bus Stop Battle in the November of this year. Traffic problems and risks to life and limb had caused a huge public outcry against the location of the bus stop in the Market Place.

This year, 1953, was memorable for the coronation of Queen Elizabeth II and for the first successful conquest of Everest by Sir Edmund Hillary and Sherpa Tensing and for Meltham Co-op Gala and Field Day of course!

At work

Left (both pictures): North Road, Kirkburton in August 1952 *(inset)* and pure nostalgia - if only traffic volumes were the same today! This shot is taken looking through Kirkburton towards the Penistone Road and an ex-government Bedford wagon can be seen driving up the middle of the road paved with 'sets'. An early Ford Anglia and a Morris van can be seen parked at the kerb on the left of this shot. The smart delivery boy, right of centre, is choosing to push rather than ride his bike up the hill, perhaps he had a heavy load. His overall, bicycle clips and the basket on the front of his bike bring back memories of butchers boys delivering the Sunday joint or a pound of sausages. The meat would often be wrapped in thin white paper with an outer packaging of brown paper which held a quickly scrawled note in the butchers hand of an abbreviation of the contents. The 'sets' are now covered in tarmac and there are changes but, nevertheless, residents of Kirkburton will recognise their village here. We've rounded the bend *(Main picture)* and this shot shows the scene further along North Road. Kirkburton, 'only gently touched by time', a picturesque Pennine village which was mentioned in the Domesday Book. A tranquil scene evocative of the peaceful post-war years. The tractor in the foreground is a Ferguson and the sun filters through the branches near to the old style bus stop sign where a young man waits for transport. Further down the road, centre of the shot, is a Shell petrol and service station with the old style petrol pumps. The building next to the petrol station, nearer to the camera, is believed to be the Kirkburton branch of the Midland Bank which opened on Wednesdays and Fridays only - and no PIN numbers, cash dispensers, credit cards or telephone banking in those days! The early fifties were eventful times. The year before this photograph was taken, 1951, Winston Churchill became Prime Minister

again and the Festival of Britain was held in London attracting visitors from all over the country including many from Huddersfield. 1952 saw the death of King George VI and the accession to the throne of Princess Elizabeth who had visited the town three years earlier. Huddersfield dressed up and partied for the coronation in June, 1953 and Sir Edmund Hillary and Sherpa Tensing were the first men to conquer Everest in the same year.

Above: A smart and gleaming pair of vehicles here - the 'Bray Fleet', the transport belonging to 'Bray for Photographs' of Cloth Hall Chambers in Huddersfield. This photograph was taken by Morris Bray in September 1951 and, at that time, Mr Bray traded in commercial, industrial and press photography. The vehicles in this shot had both started their lives as saloon cars, a 1932 Austin Ten and a 1939 Singer Super Ten. Mr Morris Bray had worked as an apprentice in the publicity department of the David Brown Organisation then, after a spell as a photographer with the Royal Navy - at the request of King George! - Mr Bray worked as a staff photographer with the Huddersfield Examiner before starting his own business in Cloth Hall Street in 1948. With an initial intention to specialise in industrial photography, Mr Bray also covered weddings and other forms of social photography. In 1962 he moved out of the town centre to specialise in industrial, architectural and general publicity photography nationwide.

The Bray family's connection with the photography business began in 1917-18 with Morris Bray's father, Mr Harry Bray and his business in Holmfirth. Mr Trevor Bray and his daughter Helen, representing the third generation of the business, still work from Holmfirth concentrating on wedding and portrait photography.

Above: An amazing feat of engineering! Lifting gear for the bridge over the canal at Turnbridge as it was in August 1952. As can be seen from the date on the enormous weight on the left, the lifting gear dates back to 1865 around eighty years after Sir John Ramsden built the canal which ultimately put Huddersfield onto the industrial map.

This photograph with its soot-blackened walls, the small house and the gas lamp to the right of the shot are truly evocative of Huddersfield's past and commercial development.

Industry, hard work, good ideas and enterprising men who had the courage to see their ideas through. A global chemicals industry began in Huddersfield with a 21 year old, Read Holliday, distilling ammonia! When Mary Hanson ran a pack-horse service between Longwood and Huddersfield could she ever have dreamed that she had started a company which would one day win a contract worth over £10 million from the company started by Read Holliday?

In the 1870s one Ben Shaw took the risk of leaving the textile industry and for £6, £3 on account and the rest by instalments, bought 'a horse and gear'. He succeeded, became one of the first users of the telephone in Huddersfield, his number was 383, had a dandelion plant as his trademark and nowadays the company is the third largest dispense company of soft drinks in Great Britain - and it all began with a wheelbarrow and a debt of £3!

Right: The weather forecast for the Huddersfield area for the weekend of May 19th 1951 was 'light easterly winds, long bright periods but risks of outbreaks of thundery rain. Moderate visibility with normal temperatures'. A reasonably good weather prospect, thankfully no gale force winds expected. An all important weather forecast because it was over this weekend that the Holme Moss TV mast was brought to its full height of 750 feet. The steel structure weighed 140 tons and was completed when eight further aerials were added a few days later. This photograph shows a workman assembling some of the parts for the mast. The base of the mast can be seen at the back of this shot, it was set on two and a half inch steel bearings and held in place by steel stay ropes. This design detail allowed the mast to move a few fractions of a degree between the cables when the wind was strong.

Radio transmissions began in May and televised broadcasts began at 10 am on August 15th 1951. Perhaps the BBC had taken Huddersfield Holiday Week into account! The Huddersfield Daily Examiner dated October 12th, 1952 listed television broadcasts as beginning at 5.45 with programmes for children and closing at 10.15 pm with the weather, news and a sound only political broadcast. The first televised children's programme is believed to have been a dramatised version of the Billy Bunter stories. The age of television had arrived and our lives and knowledge of the world and its events were changed forever.

Above and right: These photographs shows stages in the building of what was once the Jobcentre and what is now Cabletel House. This picture taken in 1973 clearly illustrates the dramatic changes which have taken place in this section of the town. Both shots show a bus parked at a shelter at the upper left hand edge. Nowadays it is likely that the bus would, of course, be found behind the large wall, upper right, the area which is now the new bus station.

Heywoods Department Store once stood on this site. Their building was sadly devasted by a spectacular fire in the 1960s which was reported widely in the local press. Spring Grove School building stands proudly on the skyline of both shots. These two photographs are rather like the puzzles found in magazines where the reader is required to 'spot the differences'. The 'stage one' picture shows us a temporary bus stop and people queuing. This has disappeared in the second stage shot but we have gained a white signboard, left of centre. Jebsons Salesrooms, Property Agents, also advertise themselves as being open in the bottom right hand corner of the second stage shot and a Hillman Imp has appeared, bottom left. Interestingly, all of the people,

apart from the building workers, have disappeared from view by Stage Two. Were they scared away having been recorded on film for posterity in their 70s gear? Gentlemen, do you remember the sideburns? Those incredibly wide flares? The wide 'kipper' ties? The pastel floral matching shirt and tie sets? No wonder these good citizens of Huddersfield have run for cover!

Above both pictures: Another 'spot the differences' challenge here. Photographs showing different stages in the building of Crown House on Southgate in 1973. Crown House is the Inland Revenue building. Looking down the road in the foreground to the left, we are looking towards Shore Head Roundabout and the University.

The 'Stage One' shot shows the chimney of Brierley's mill, still there today, slightly left of centre and a clear view of the Huddersfield Sports Centre behind the construction site. At the left hand edge is a corner of a block of flats, one of the three blocks named Richmond, Ibbotson and Lonsborough.

Citizens of Huddersfield can be justly proud of the athletic achievements of their world champions Derek Ibbotson and Anita Lonsborough. Derek Ibbotson broke the world mile record in 1957 with a time of 3 minutes 57 seconds and Anita Lonsborough won gold medals in both Olympic and European swimming competitions. Both shots show the old telephone exchange building at the right hand edge of the frame and the new Sainsbury's store is just off these shots to the right.

WC Holmes & Co can be seen upper left of the 'Stage Two' shot and travelling along the road in the foreground are an old Mini Countryman, a Bedford van and could the wagon be a Thomas Trader?

The background view in both shots is looking across the valley towards Kilner Bank and beyond lies Dalton. Huddersfield Broad Canal - Ramsden Canal - runs along the back of this photograph and, on the stage one shot, the street between the mill buildings, right of centre, is the location of the old lifting bridge, still there and dating back to the construction of the canal.

Below: The beginnings of the construction of the Digley Reservoir at Holmbridge in April 1952. At the time this photograph was taken engineers were anticipating the collection of water in the new reservoir in three or four months time to test out the construction. The local press reported a 'sufficiency' of labour but a shortage of skilled workers in particular pitchers, quarrymen and masons. Readers may remember the old Isle of Skye public house which was closed and demolished in the 1950s due to pollution risks to the new Digley Reservoir.

In 1952 we all drank water from the tap, we'd never heard of Perrier. Housewives had 'turned to Tide for the cleanest wash of all'. Tide came in a colourful box with a design of concentric circles and the word 'Tide' written boldly across them. Oxydol would, of course, have claimed that they would give you the cleanest wash of all! And if bending over the 'peggy tub', turning the mangle and using the rubbing board gave you backache you could always take Doans pills. They would cure backache for 1s 7d - around 8p. If you felt a little down in the dumps Phensic could cure depression and soothe nerves. You could take a break from cooking and open a tin for tea, how about 'sweet tender prunes ready to serve' at 2/- a tin (10p). Or, in order to 'gain full health and that graceful holiday charm' - BILE BEANS at 1s 9d or 4s for a large pack (9p or 20p). Readers would probably gladly part with 20p in order to gain full health and that graceful holiday charm! Why not throw caution to the winds and take a day excursion to the Great

Yorkshire Show in Harrogate with Yorkshire Traction Buses for 5s 9d return (29p). Well, maybe once in a Holmfirth flood?

Right: There has been an astonishing rate of technological advances in this century and particularly in the last fifty years. Could our parents have ever envisaged a computer in the home? E-mail? A washing machine that, with the turn of a switch, changes oily or muddy overalls into immaculately clean and dry clothing ready to wear again? Cinemas have not escaped the advances in technology and this photograph illustrates one of the major changes. The projection rooms of cinemas used to employ several members of staff. The machinery in this photograph shows why that is no longer the case. The shot was taken at the ABC Cinema on Market Street in Huddersfield in February, 1974 when the ABC converted its magnificent 2,000 seat auditorium into two smaller cinemas and a public house -The Painted Wagon. In front of the technician in this picture, nearer to the camera, is a two tier unit known as 'the cake stand'. The technicians splice up all the relevant film, the main feature, the news item, advertisements and 'trailers', and the whole evening's entertainment runs from one tier onto the other with cues to control the lights, open and close the curtains. The entire work for that evening becomes one seamless piece of technology and all designed to run 'unmanned'. But it can't sell the ice cream!

in to help but no trace of the murder weapon could be found. Moore was convicted at Leeds Assizes on the evidence of the dying policeman and was executed. These photographs show the police and the army around the farm on the Sunday morning after the shootings and Moore's arrest.

Above: The ICI Chemical complex in Huddersfield as seen from Dalton Bank Road in May 1973. Huddersfield has been described as 'the cradle of the chemicals industry' and it is easy to see why. The chemicals industry has become

Left both pictures: On a Saturday night in July 1951 the police had arranged a 'stake-out' around a farm in Cockley Hill, Kirkheaton the home of one Alfred Moore. Inspector Duncan Fraser of the Huddersfield Division of the West Yorkshire Constabulary and Constable Arthur Jagger who was based in Slaithewaite were the officers on duty, watching the farm throughout the night. At around 2 am the two police officers are understood to have spoken to a man in a field near to Cockley Hill Lane. It is believed that some kind of altercation followed during which Inspector Fraser was shot dead instantly by three bullets entering his body. PC Jagger was shot in the lower part of his body. Other police officers in the area heard the shots and summoned help for their colleagues and reinforcements for themselves. The police believed that a man had entered Whinney Close Farm and subsequently armed policemen took up watch on the farmhouse. The police maintained their vigil until daylight when they began to close in. At around 5.30 that morning a man came from the house and spoke to the police. He was later seen by neighbours to have been led away handcuffed to a policeman.

After an operation, PC Jagger regained consciousness and was able to assist his colleagues in identifying the man who had shot Inspector Fraser and himself. An identification parade of eight men wearing raincoats was held at his hospital bedside where a special court also charged Alfred Moore. Moore was taken to and from Huddersfield Infirmary in a black police van and covered his head in a raincoat. Mrs Jagger spent all day with her husband who died the following morning. Moore was subsequently charged with the murder of PC Jagger and faced the double murder charge on the following day having been detained in Huddersfield.

The shootings had taken place in a field which was reported by the press as being 'a foot deep in mowing grass'. Immediately it was daylight a minute search was made of the exact spot where the policemen had fallen and then the rest of the field. A coachload of policemen brought in from other divisions arrived to assist with the search. Two police dogs, an alsatian and a labrador, and their handlers were brought

interwoven with the working lives of Huddersfield families throughout most of the twentieth century. In 1830 an enterprising young man by the name of Read Holliday set himself up in the business of distilling ammonia. He was 21 and traded out of premises in Tanfield, off Leeds Road. Nine years later, in 1839, he had been so successful that a move to Turnbridge, near to the Huddersfield Gas Light Company on the east of the town had become possible. By this time Read Holliday and Sons were concentrating on the distillation of Coal Tar, which at the time was considered a waste product of gas production. Out of this so called waste came products such as ammonia, creosote, benzene and paint solvents.

1914 saw an urgent expansion in the dyestuffs industry to meet wartime needs and British Dyes Ltd was formed from Read Holliday and Sons with help from the government and the substantial and well known site on Leeds Road was acquired. By 1919 the British Dyestuffs Corporation had been founded after amalgamation with Levinstein Ltd and by 1926 the company had become ICI - a name that was to become synonymous with Huddersfield and with famous products such as Nylon and Terylene.

Later years were to see Zeneca and ICI become entirely separate companies with Zeneca still operating out of Huddersfield along with many other sites around the country. Zeneca trade in three main areas, pharmaceuticals, agro-chemicals and speciality chemicals whilst ICI's stock in trade was in plastics, acrylics and petro-chemicals. ICI is now a much smaller company than Zeneca and has sites mostly dotted around the north of England with their head office in London. The name Zeneca is intriguing - why Zeneca? There are a range of potential answers to that question. One is that the name was based on the Greek word for excellence or highest achievement. It has also been suggested that Zeneca means absolutely nothing in any language in the world today and so can be used everywhere without risk of embarrassment! Another that with an initial letter 'Z' Zeneca would always be noticed in stock market listings. Take your Pick as Michael Miles used to say. The truth is probably, as it invariably is, a combination of all those things.

Isn't this a lovely sight? There is something special about horse-drawn transport, a charm that motorised vehicles will never have - and they can't provide for the roses in the same way!

The nowadays global Hanson business empire has always had a connection with horses. The company began with Mary and Joseph Hanson on the cobbled streets of Longwood in the mid 1800s and their pack horse service carrying wool and textiles between Longwood and Huddersfield.

This picture was taken in Cloth Hall Street in 1958 but this horse-drawn vehicle could be seen around town well into the 1960s.

In 1951, The Huddersfield Examiner carried an article sub-titled 'Hansons and Horses' and reported that the Hansons had an almost unbroken record of show successes and that, since the end of the war, had won no less than 132 awards. This particular article featured Unique owned by Mr Robert Hanson and regarded as the best middle-weight hunter in the land.

The same edition of the Examiner carried a large advertisement offering a £1,000 reward for information which would establish the whereabouts of one Donald Maclean and one Guy Burgess. The reward was offered by the Daily Express and the quarter-page advertisement carried sketches of both men. The rewards was being offered to 'any person who sends to the Daily Express definite evidence that will lead to the solution of the most puzzling mystery in recent years'. Readers will no doubt remember that Burgess and Maclean were spying for the Russians and being tipped off by Philby that they were likely to be caught, made a run for cover in the Soviet Union where they were treated as heroes and lived out the rest of their lives.